THE COLOR OF THE NIGHT

REFLECTIONS ON THE BOOK OF JOB

GERHARD E. FROST

AUGSBURG PUBLISHING HOUSE
MINNEAPOLIS, MINNESOTA

THE COLOR OF THE NIGHT

Copyright © 1977 Augsburg Publishing House

Library of Congress Catalog Card No. 77-72458

International Standard Book No. 0-8066-1583-4

Scripture quotations are from the Revised Standard Version of the Bible, copyright 1946, 1952, and 1971 by the Division of Christian Education of the National Council of Churches.

MANUFACTURED IN THE UNITED STATES OF AMERICA

To Ivern.

We have heard

the morning stars sing together.

THE COLOR OF THE NIGHT

Preface

"Grandma?"

"Yes?"

"It's been a bad day, a really bad day! I lost my best friend, and the teacher made me sit by myself because she thought I talked too much. On my way home I made a snowball, and I threw it, and I told God I hoped it hit him right in the heart! But after a while I told him I was sorry, and then things got a little better."

A starkly honest telephone report of a day in the life of a seven-year-old. A one-minute, dramatic summary of the Book of Job.

Job made more than a snowball, and he threw it all at God. He didn't doubt God's existence, but he tortured himself over whether God was for or against him.

I, too, have made my snowball and thrown it at God. But I have heard the good news, and I believe there is more than power and intelligence behind this world. There is love. There is heart. Everything happening on this broken planet with its sin-battered children hits God right in the heart.

The Color of the Night? I came to the title by a circuitous route.

It was the last week in a Lenten season. The place was a charming little church set in a wooded village in northern New Jersey. During Lent I had preached on the seven words of Christ from the cross and had followed services with adult forums on the Book of Job. As barriers went down and new friendships were formed, several members of the class shared confidences with the group.

On this evening one member began to recount certain crises which her family was going through. Prompted by her honesty, I broke in and said, "I must tell you that I would be the worst of pretenders if I claimed to have things under control. I know the color of the night!"

On my way home I reflected how often I had struggled with ways to characterize the essence of the Book of Job. How could I have claimed so earnestly to "know" the color of the night, a knowledge Job himself wrestled with in trials far beyond any I'd experienced?

Can it be that Job shares with me, with my friend, with you, too, different perceptions of a night that blankets all? I invite you to look with me into Job's night, and into mine and yours. What color is it? Does it hold a star? A rainbow? A presence? Let us join hearts and minds in the search.

The Book of Job suffers much from prevailing misconceptions. The rumor is abroad that Job is a docile fellow, a bundle of boils and questions who takes his lickings without a whimper, the very epitome of patience. And who wants patience?

The truth is that Job is one of God's spirited children. But his pluck and spirit can't be explained on the basis of raw courage or any other human quality. Job's outrage stemmed from his unshakable conviction that God has integrity in his dealings with people. In fact, God's integrity is on trial in the story of Job.

Why reflect on the Book of Job? Because it nourishes

our sense of wonder and helps us live with mystery, enabling us to let God be God, even during his silences.

We reflect on Job to deepen our level of inquiry and to share more fully in the asking of life's disturbing questions, to keep from mouthing simplistic solutions and to avoid the impertinence of "arriving" without making the journey.

We reflect also to consider the perennial clash between frozen dogma and personal pain in the always unpredictable human situation.

Finally, we reflect to better understand the struggle between faith and feelings, hoping to live less fearfully and more openly with suffering and with sufferers, that we may face more honestly the limitations of human counsel and be drawn into new and significant dialog with persons who are often misunderstood and avoided.

What is this Book of Job? It has been called the Matterhorn of the Old Testament. Just as a mountain commands respect, so with the Book of Job. Its peaks are high, its valleys deep, and its trails many. It keeps its secret well, even as it offers signs. It doesn't deal with a single problem, and it isn't an answer book. Rather, it illumines all of life by revealing, at the end, the God who gives himself in power and love to the weary. It addresses the yearning of the human heart as seen through the anguish of one good man.

The universality of Job lies in his struggle with inescapable perplexities which torture us all, especially those involved in the life of faith. Job presents, not a touched-up portrait of how the tested person ought to act, but rather a candid shot of how a person does act when pain is intense and protracted.

Job's torment is perhaps best exhibited in two utterances of Christ from his cross: "My God, my God, why hast thou forsaken me?" and "Father, into thy hands I commit my spirit!" Like other Old Testament characters, Job cries for Christ.

There was a man

There was a man in the land of
Uz, whose name was Job (1:1).

The road winds; it is a country road. I see a plowman against the setting sun. I lift my hand as I speed by; he lifts his, in ancient ritual.

"Hypocrite, to wave at one unknown to you, and you to him!" So says the cynic in my soul.

To salute humanity and so confess that I was born and I, too, must die? It is not too much, nor is it false, between two mortals who dream one dream—the dream of loving and of being loved.

His name was Job

There was a man . . . whose name
was Job (1:1).

Four words reach for me: "There was a man." They excite me to reflect and to expect. Four more, "whose name was Job," have the makings of a story. And I have the feeling that this is my story, your story, every person's story.

Always there are persons—persons with names and a story—in danger of being lost. Bent, flattened stapled, and filed, we lose each other in statistics and generalizations, triplicate forms and nine-digit numbers. We let the question become academic, hiding the questioner. We permit the garment to muffle the beating heart within. We don't feel that pounding pulse of the person, that person with a name.

The Book of Job is about a person almost unheard, pressed to the wall by unbearable mystery, a person who "walked beside our race" impaled on the spearpoint of human doubts and longings.

The book testifies to the truth that people are God's purpose. It is a classic story of birth, life, death, and destiny. Therefore it begins where it must begin. "There was a man whose name was Job."

The greatest of all

And that man was blameless and upright,
one who feared God, and turned away from evil.
There were born to him seven sons and three
daughters. He had seven thousand sheep, three
thousand camels, five hundred yoke of oxen,
and five hundred she-asses, and very many
servants; so that this man was the greatest of all
the people of the east (1:1b-3).

Job, the complete man, lives a balanced, proportioned, many-sided life. He stands tall in any crowd, "like a tree planted by streams of water," the ornament of the forest.

This is God's man in the world, husband and father, property owner and community leader, champion of the weak and friend of the poor. No grass grows on the path to his door, for many feet trample it. Here is a man respected, listened to, and loved.

This biblical picture of the complete person speaks of relationships. Job doesn't fulfill himself by turning inward. He is meant to know and to make himself known by the outreach of his life and his interlocking connections with the world around him.

Walk in the forest when the storm is past and see how seldom a branch is broken except where it connects with the trunk or another branch. Character is most severely tested at the point of relationship. This is where storms tear and torture both trees and human beings.

Tested, but true

That man was blameless and upright, one who
feared God, and turned away from evil (1:1).

At first glance Job appears to be true, but untested. Yet
he has been stringently tested—he has lived with prosperity. The Lord has offered him the challenges of great
wealth. He has burdened this tree with the weight of much
fruit.

Doesn't the sunny day determine what happens in the
storm? Hard moments don't make us; they measure us.
It is in quiet weather that our lives are shaped as we
commit ourselves to the true or the false.

Our ways of saying "I" and "me" and "my" express
our ultimate treasons and devotions. "The satanically
managed man," says Oswald Chambers, "is moral, upright, proud and individual; he is absolutely self-governed
and has no need for God."

Job has remained childlike before his God. His gift-
consciousness is strong and healthy. He acknowledges his
dependence and knows in whom to trust.

16

The person prepared

*His sons used to go and hold a feast, and when
the days of the feast had run their course, Job
would send and sanctify them. Thus Job did
continually (from 1:4-5).*

Isn't the stuff of life in the common and the repeated?
Aren't the dimensions of a life revealed in what is done
"continually"? Aren't we best described in terms of our
habits?

Job, "the greatest of all the people of the east," is great
with that greatness which begins at home. Although his
supporting community stretches to distant places, he is
respected most by those who know him best.

It isn't preparation for life, but participation in it, that
makes us strong for the storm. There is no rehearsal, no
waiting line. All is participation. Job, the person prepared, lives fully in his family and larger community.
This is his integrity and his strength.

That day

Now there was a day ... (1:6).

Every day moves toward the crucial day which exposes what one has become. For Job there have been many days of living on the sunny side of the hill. The critical nature of these days was hidden by the trappings of affluence and outward success. Superficially, Job appeared a person without a problem, young in spirit and in years, accustomed to counsel and command. See him, this Job, moving surely and confidently, unchastened, untempered, untamed.

But "now there was a day"!

There are no neutral moments. Time is alive with the hidden drama of choice and decision. Life moves. Always and everywhere each person is taking shape in relation to "that day."

My servant

*And the Lord said to Satan, "Have you
considered my servant Job, that there is none
like him on earth, a blameless and upright man,
who fears God and turns away from evil?" (1:8).*

"My servant Job." To pass over these words lightly
is to be locked out of the deeper meanings of the book.

We will say many things about this person, Job, but
all of them are insignificant when balanced against this
three-word verdict, this stamp of integrity issuing from
God. Here the Lord speaks his authoritative "mine." This
is grace.

Grace flows through the entire Book of Job. It is the
hidden stream, the strong current, that carries and controls
the story. God's loving favor reigns in Job's life, even
when he is shrouded with silence.

He holds me

"Have you considered my servant Job?" (1:8b).

To know who and whose we are is the first preparation for the untried and unknown. We are mysteries to one another and to ourselves, but one thing we can and must know. We must know to whom we belong.

Dietrich Bonhoeffer, from behind prison walls, raised the lonely question, "Who am I?" He considered the contradictory answers of others in the light of what he saw in himself. To others he appeared strong, serene, sufficient; to himself, sick, empty, weary. But in all this his trembling faith affirmed, "Whoever I am, Thou knowest, O Lord, I am Thine!"

Job couldn't hear what we are hearing on his behalf, and this is the essence of his struggle. In the loving and cherishing words "my servant Job," we see the initiative of the Lord as he reaches out to claim and hold his own.

I won't forget a moment of self-accusation and anxiety which I experienced many years ago while crossing a busy intersection with our four-year-old. My arms filled with two bags of groceries, I told him to take hold of my coat pocket and not to let go. Halfway across the street I realized how unwise I had been. At a moment of panic the child could have let go. Of course, I should have held his hand. Reflecting on this, I have thought of God's commitment to me. He holds me with the love that will not let me go!

Have you considered?

And the Lord said to Satan,
"Have you considered my servant?" (1:8).

It jolts us to see the Lord deliberately single out Job and challenge the adversary to test him. Why does God mark his servant for suffering? The Lord knows his own; therefore he knows Job is gold. He understands how his children can best be sustained.

God never permits loss except to make room for greater gain. He impoverishes only to ultimately enrich. He not only wants to fill us; he aims to enlarge us. He stretches us to receive him.

The testing of Job will enrich many. Our greatest teachers are often the greatest sufferers, not because they have been given all the answers, but because they have experienced the Presence.

Confess the mystery

"Have you considered . . ." (1:8).

It is both superficial and dishonest to presume to fully understand God's purpose in the life of any Job, ancient or contemporary. We view with faith, not sight, the unequal circumstances in the lives of people we know. The Lord's ways are veiled.

At this moment we cannot see the beginning and the end. We can't, like God, know all things in one act of knowing. We must therefore begin by confessing the mystery circumscribing all knowledge, sustaining and framing all inquiry. This mystery is inexhaustible, more vast the more one knows.

Yet exploring the unfathomable is not to be discouraged. The trails skirting God's mysteries are meant to be our temporal home. We forsake them at the expense of our humanity. We dare not live even in the outskirts of life's fierce questions without confessing and ultimately celebrating those mysteries which carry us beyond all explaining.

Satan's slander

*Then Satan answered the Lord, "Does Job fear
God for naught? Hast thou not put a hedge
about him and his house and all that he has,
on every side? Thou hast blessed the work of
his hands, and his possessions have increased
in the land. But put forth thy hand now, and
touch all that he has, and he will curse thee to
thy face." And the Lord said to Satan, "Behold,
all that he has is in your power; only upon
himself do not put forth your hand." So Satan
went forth from the presence of the Lord
(1:9-12).*

The adversary, Satan, now appears as a roving spirit,
ceaselessly active in aggressive assault on all who, like Job,
are in the company of God's servants. His question "Does
Job fear God for naught?" exposes the very nerve of the
book. Everything hinges on the answer.

Is there true worship on earth? In the case of Job, the
Lord issues a challenge in the words "my servant." Are
these words true? Does the Lord create faith and establish
relationship? Is he able to elicit sincere worship, or is all
so-called devotion nothing more than fear-motivated ex-
pediency? Is all service and obedience only a kind of
slave morality? Is there such a thing as human freedom,
or are we, as the behaviorists maintain, conditioned by
reward and punishment?

"Does Job fear God for naught?" This is the permanent front line of the Book of Job, the focal conflict and ultimate slander. It slanders the Lord before it touches Job. God is the main character in this story. In New Testament terms, the question becomes: Is the Christian community sustained by love? Is there reality in the body of Christ as faith affirms it? Is the Holy Spirit truly at work in the creation of new beings, reclaiming persons for God? In short, does God have integrity?

The adversary appears as more than a tester of people. He has a quarrel with God, and it is not a lover's quarrel. His question is a sniper's bullet, intended to undermine and destroy. His strategy is to blend truth with falsehood by insinuation and innuendo.

There is truth in the assertion that the Lord has "put a hedge about" Job and "blessed the work of his hands." It is true, too, that the Lord has many false friends and that there is much hypocrisy in us all. But this is not the whole truth about Job or about us. All of God's servants aren't cheap opportunists whose faith is mere superstition and whose religion is all in the purse. God does continue to create and sustain his family in our very midst. This is the continued story.

But God is still God

*And the Lord said to Satan, "Behold,
all that he has is in your power, only upon
himself do not put forth your hand" (1:12).*

God sets limits to the testing of Job. Satan isn't given the throne. We would be in utter confusion and despair if the Lord did not say, "Only upon himself do not put forth your hand." How crushing to feel, in times of stress, that God is no longer God! Sometimes we mistake hiddenness for abandonment. Even when our feelings testify against us, we can remember what we know—that God is faithful, that his waiting isn't weakness and his silence isn't desertion.

God neither abdicates nor is dethroned. The long tunnels and frightening eclipses we encounter are not without God's loving presence and merciful power. Our "total losses" cannot include the loss of our Lord.

Naked!

*Then Job arose, and rent his robe, and shaved
his head, and fell upon the ground,
and worshiped (1:20).*

"So Satan went forth from the presence of the
Lord. . . ." Here occurs an ominous break in the dialog,
followed by the swift and furious unfolding of a story of
loss upon loss, until Job is left with neither property nor
children.

"Then Job arose, and rent his robe, and shaved his
head, and fell upon the ground, and worshiped." After a
devastating storm has swept through a forest, one knows
each tree by a new revelation. "I had no idea that this
one was rotting here," we say, or, "See, this one isn't
damaged at all!" In the one word "worshiped" we have
a new revelation of Job. He doesn't break because he can
bend.

"Naked I came from my mother's womb, and naked
shall I return; the Lord gave, and the Lord has taken
away; blessed be the name of the Lord." Here Job takes
his place among the "terrible meek," those strong ones
of the stormy past. To believe in the toughness and resilience of God's love is to take into oneself some of that
same resilience and strength. Job's strength lies in his consciousness of life as gift and in his obeisance to the power
of the Giver.

Skin for skin

Again there was a day when the sons
of God came to present themselves
before the Lord (2:1).

"Again there was a day"—another day, another and
fiercer test. Sometimes life is like that—no relief, just
cumulative and intensified grief when we can scarcely
endure what is.

Job has stood the first test, proving Satan's slander to
be a lie. He is, indeed, the Lord's servant. Then the ther-
mostat is reset; the refining heat is increased. This time
the adversary is less subtle. He directly contradicts the
Lord: "Skin for skin! All that a man has will he give for
his life. But put forth your hand now and touch his bone
and his flesh, and he will curse thee to thy face."

True, health is the best wealth. "If you've got your
health you've got just about everything," says the TV
commercial. "All that a man has will he give for his life."
But the Lord again stands guard over the person and
life of Job.

Note Satan's nasty implication that Job has weathered
the blows simply out of indifference to the sufferings of
others, raising a second question concerning God's integrity in creating disciples: Is there such a thing as genuine
love between human beings?

Alone among the ashes

So Satan went forth from the presence of the
Lord, and afflicted Job with loathsome sores
from the sole of his foot to the crown of his
head. And he took a potsherd with which to
scrape himself, and sat among the ashes (2:7-8).

He had much to lose, this "greatest of all the people of
the east," and now he had lost it all. Banished to the city
dump, he stirs the ashes and, in a pitiable gesture of
futility, clutches a piece of broken pottery, vainly trying
to relieve the unrelenting pain of his loathsome sores.

The attractive one has become repulsive. He to whose
door the many beat a path is now shunned and ostra-
cized, avoided by those he assisted, forsaken by those he
befriended. He who has held much in his hand and many
at his command is now not even a face in the crowd.
Alone among the ashes, Job becomes a symbol of refuse—
that which is spent, finished, used up!

Can it be that already, so early in the story, this Book
of Job is shaping a theology of the cross? Is this the end
of triumph, this hunched figure on the ash heap, this good
man who has "done everything right" and yet suffers in
the end? Must there be dying before rising, losing before
finding? Must we be stripped before we can be clothed?
Perhaps this is the reason the early church prescribed the
Book of Job as Passion Week reading—but we run ahead
of our story.

Curse God, and die

Then his wife said to him, "Do
you still hold fast your integrity?
Curse God, and die" (2:9).

We know little about Job's wife, but some things can
be assumed. She is deeply involved in each of Job's losses.
His lost property and children had been hers, too. His
anguish of spirit must incite her own inner turmoil.

At what point does her faith falter? We can't tell, but
now she offers counsel of desperation. Her suggestion
may arise not from indifference but rather from despairing
love. Perhaps she is saying something like this: "Oh,
dear Job, you've always been such a searcher. For your
own peace of mind, and mine, too, stop raising your brave
but useless questions. Don't torment yourself with painful
whys. Give up. Forsake your search for meaning. Don't
torture yourself over what God is trying to accomplish
with you."

This is attractive counsel. It becomes Job's "temptation
in the wilderness," for it invites him to enjoy the fasci-
nation of nothingness. It is tempting to look over the edge
of the nihilistic abyss and forsake the quest for dignity
and meaning. If one can cease one's inner struggle, even
with such spurious peace, one can temporarily ease one's
pain.

But Job refuses the anesthetic and chooses rather the

armor of gratitude: "Shall we receive good at the hand of God, and shall we not receive evil?"

It is a pity that Job has traditionally been associated with spiritless acquiescence and docility. He should rather be identified as the heroic wrestler, the faithful enquirer who steadfastly rejects surrender and refuses to settle back into resignation and defeat. The "patience of Job" is struggle all the way, the patience of one who grapples with apparent contradictions and wrests his comfort from painful paradox.

Let the day perish

*After this Job opened his mouth and cursed
the day of his birth. And Job said, "Let the
day perish when I was born, and the night
which said, 'A man-child is conceived!' Let that
day be darkness!" (3:1-4a).*

From the prose prolog (Chapters 1 and 2) to the
opening lines of the poem (Chapter 3), Job takes a pre-
cipitous plunge from obedient trust to radical despair. The
change is so extreme that many speak of two Jobs, the
Job of the prose prolog and epilog and the Job of the
poem. The inspired poet now turns the plot inward and
probes the crosscurrents of the sufferer's soul-struggle.

Job breaks the silence, not with an address to his friends
or even with a direct cry to God, but with a searing soliloquy, releasing his pent-up feelings of loneliness and be-
trayal. He doesn't curse God as Satan said he would; he
rather curses the day of his birth and cries for release from
life. He pours out his envy of the dead, the stillborn, and
the neverborn. Life for Job has become nothing more than
unbearable pain. His fear of life is greater than his fear of
death, so he pleads for nothingness.

One of the perils of wealth is that it offers something
to hide in. Job has "dressed" in his wealth; his possessions
and position have hidden his nakedness as a person. The
satin curtain has remained intact. Now his sufferings un-
dress him to his very center and reveal his total helplessness.

Why?

"Why did I not die at birth? Why did the knees receive me? Or why the breasts, that I should suck? Or why was I not as a hidden untimely birth, as infants that never see the light? Why is light given to him that is in misery, and life to the bitter in soul? Why is light given to a man whose way is hid, whom God has hedged in?" (from 3:11-23).

Six *whys*, arrows from the quiver of darkness, have pierced the heart of Job, and now he lets his anger erupt in that aching, hollow word.

With the turbulence of a volcano, Job's hot *whys* tumble over each other. "Why was I not stillborn? Why did my father and mother pledge to care for me when this is the terrifying outcome? Why was I brought this far when the road leads to a dead end?" Job sees himself as God's tragic blunder. He asks to be blotted out.

Our first impulse may be to say, "How melodramatic, how untrue to my life!" But don't we, too, know moments when we hurl our No! into the face of God? Aren't there times of "too much," when we feel trapped by the sheer weight of circumstance? If we don't literally damn the day of our birth, don't our complaints against God and our arguments with him become loud and angry within us? "I wish I'd never been born!" Or, if we don't reject life outright, we may reject our own: "Why wasn't I someone else?"

Surely no one of mature years is a stranger to Job's wilderness of despair. One of the deadliest and most constant temptations is to live by negation rather than by affirmation, to withdraw from courageous participation and turn one's face to the wall.

Job loses his head because he has given his heart. The intensity of his struggle is evidence of the depth of his commitment. Perhaps God takes more pleasure in the child who shakes a fist at heaven than in one who sulks and never looks up. I am reminded of a recent conversation with one whose faith I deeply respect. Frustrated, this person said about God, "But lately I've mostly been yelling at him!" Job yells at God because he cares.

For us, there are still those reassuring words, "my servant," which Job couldn't hear. There is the open road, blazed not by the courage of human heroes, but by the faithfulness of a loving God. To follow this road is to know that the heart's adventure is not in human quest but in encounter with the divine.

Why such mystery?

*"Why is light given to a man whose way
is hid, whom God hedges in?" (3:23).*

The spearpoint of Job's many questions is this: Why
so much mystery? Why must I travel blind?

This is one of the most profound levels of pain. Job's
outcry is more than protest against the anguish of isola-
tion and the loss of his supporting community. It is the
supreme agony that comes from trying to make sense of
that which lies beyond the reach of logic. It is a crisis in
meaning. Job feels himself to be in the grip of ultimate
nonsense. His cry is qualitatively above the *whys* of intellectual inquiry. It is a religious outcry, a protest against
life's unyielding absurdity, against the incoherence of his
situation.

We are meant for this reflective warfare. This is our
dignity. We are exploring, probing, searching, and reach-
ing creatures. We are God's hurting ones. Amid the mag-
nificence of Who? What? How? Where? and When? is
the ennobling Why? It must never cease to be asked.

We must raise our *whys*. And we will, whether we
wish to or not. The mind can no more contain its whys
than the body can hold its breath. But there are many
ways of asking why. It can be whined or cursed or snarled
or pouted. But it can also be prayed.

A why can be a child's empty cup, held up to the love
and wisdom of our gracious God. Our Lord doesn't fill it

to the brim, but he satisfies each person's need. He is too kind to drown us in all the knowledge we crave. He doesn't give more than we can hold; sometimes we must wait to be made larger cups. Our present questions may be the wrong ones. Then he helps us outgrow them and prompts us to move on to better ones.

God knows that the road we must travel would overwhelm us if we could, in a single moment, see around every bend. He gives us a candle rather than a floodlight—and he promises to be there. He asks us to remember that mystery is one form of his mercy. His aim is not to keep things from us, but to keep things—the best things—for us!

Who can
keep from speaking?

Then Eliphaz, the Temanite, answered:
"If one ventures a word with you, will you
be offended? Yet, who can keep from
speaking?" (4:1-2).

Job, the "greatest of all the people of the east," has influential and prominent friends, among them Eliphaz, Bildad, and Zophar. These men hear the report of Job's misfortunes with concern and come from afar to console him. They come promptly to provide a supporting community in this time of distress.

Though expecting to find a critical situation, these friends are shocked by what they see. They are compelled to observe a ritual silence in token of the hopelessness of Job's condition.

Job's friends are trapped in the narrow belief that suffering corresponds directly to the sinfulness of the sufferer. This, the orthodox position in those times, is undoubtedly shared by Job. The heresy has persisted through the time of Christ to our very day. We often hear someone say, "What have I done, that this should happen to me?"

During the long silence, those who came to sympathize and console Job have shaped a judgment against him. Compassion has given way to condemnation. Now the moment has arrived for Eliphaz, the eldest and most prestigious, to bring in the report.

Lost among the many

*"Behold, you have instructed many, and you
have strengthened the weak hands. Your words
have upheld him who was stumbling, and you
have made firm the feeble knees. But now it has
come to you, and you are impatient; it touches
you, and you are dismayed. Is not your fear of
God your confidence, and the integrity of
your ways your hope?" (4:3-6).*

Eliphaz isn't a gross character. Intending to be gentle,
he begins carefully, with a little preamble to cushion what
he is about to say. But he speaks as one whose mind is
made up. He neither asks nor listens. His attack is thinly
veiled. Perhaps in a more manageable situation he would
be considerate and sensitive, but, like us, when drawn
beyond his depth he becomes cruel.

Interpretations of the speeches of Job's three friends
vary, but on one thing they agree: love is missing. The
counselors don't try to hear Job. They rush past him
and run over him, ignoring him as a person. "You have
instructed many. . . . But now it has come to you." Job
has become a statistic, one of the "many." "It" has happened to you. This is a damning word because it speaks
in generalization, and love refuses to generalize. The word
it, so innocent on the surface, loses Job in the mass and
robs him of individuality.

Generalizations are easy, too easy. We come to them

without effort and express them in cheap talk. Nevertheless, they are the common language of heartlessness among "good" people.

To love a person is first to let that person "be," to offer living room. Eliphaz is guilty of failure to show such respect. He loses Job and never finds him again.

Love's first gift is attention. Its first and hardest work is listening. A child runs to his mother, not to tell her how much burns hurt, but to tell her how much "my burn" hurts. Love bends low and waits long to hear the story of another's pain.

When the sufferer isn't heard, violence occurs. The child's tantrum is the language of a small person who is unheard or misunderstood. The riot is an expression of a community of the ignored. Every suffering is new, without duplicate or stereotype. Therefore, it is the genius of love to "see things new."

Eliphaz is the moralist from the outset. His first "gentle" word is a judgment. He comes, not as friend, but as judge and theologian with something to prove. In human need, the lover must run ahead of the logician, for the heart blazes trails where there is no road for the mind. God would love his world through us.

As I have seen

"Think now, who that was innocent ever perished? As I have seen, those who plow iniquity and sow trouble reap the same. By the breath of God they perish, and by the blast of his anger they are consumed" (4:7-9).

Eliphaz and his friends, handcuffed by their narrow creed, are unequipped to cope with mystery as it is embodied in the suffering Job. They are too brittle to change.

Faced with alternatives, to rewrite their "catechism" or to reject Job, they choose the latter. Instead of recognizing an invitation to advance into the unknown and join Job's faith-struggle, they retreat into the fancied safety of their rigid position.

Great courage is required to share a human predicament which lies beyond explanation. Retreat is tempting. Hearing another's story requires patience, courage, and love. It forces us to scuttle every easy answer and ready solution.

Now Job joins the masses of the unheard. This is the central pathos of the book. But we, too, are reluctant to lay down our preachments. We would rather make speeches to a rejected one than receive him and be left speechless.

I know
just how you feel

"As I have seen . . ." (4:8).

Eliphaz fancies that he understands. He thinks he has "been there." So now he violates his friend by pretending familiarity with his pain.

Casting himself in the role of "the honest man," Eliphaz sets out on the road of presumption and falsehood by forgetting that we don't walk in each other's shoes. "The heart knows its own bitterness and a stranger does not intermeddle with its joys."

The moment I say, "I know just how you feel," I make myself a liar. I forfeit the hurting one's confidence when I claim too much. The highest understanding is to admit that I cannot fully understand.

We are most inclined toward extravagant claims when we have lived through experiences similar to those of the suffering one, but we do well to remember the wisdom of Wallace Stevens:

> Twenty men crossing a bridge,
> Into a village,
> Are twenty men crossing twenty bridges,
> Into twenty villages.

Every place of pain is a place of revelation. It is holy ground to sufferer and counselor alike, and sometimes the only appropriate gift is just to be there.

For your good

"Can mortal man be righteous before God?
Can a man be pure before his Maker? . . . Lo,
this we have searched out; it is true. Hear,
and know it for your good" (4:17; 5:27).

Eliphaz is shocked. He and his companions are over-whelmed by the dimensions of Job's predicament. Wishing to create distance between himself and the problem, Eliphaz attempts to silence Job by stirring his sense of guilt. He bludgeons him with ancient axioms, beautiful and unanswerable, but irrelevant to Job's situation.

In stressing that he has searched the nights and days for answers, Eliphaz reveals that he is unaware of how far Job, impelled by pain, has outstripped his friends in the search for meaning. He doesn't sufficiently respect Job's exposure in the school of solitude and silence.

We become irrelevant in a sitution of pain if we fail to recognize in the sufferer our best-accredited teacher. Eliphaz' address shows that beautiful words can be ineffectual and even satanic if they lack the credentials of love.

Get right with God

"As for me, I would seek God, and to God I would commit my cause; who does great things and unsearchable, marvelous things without number" (5:9).

Now, with loveless orthodoxy, Eliphaz further lacerates Job's wounds by turning him in upon himself. With insensitivity born of his sense of inadequacy, Eliphaz says, in effect: "Job, what you need is to get right with God. Take a closer look at yourself. Examine your prayer life; see if there isn't something missing. Fine-comb your past."

But more of Job is the last thing Job needs. He already has too much of himself on his hands. The weight of it is crushing him. The advice of Eliphaz adds to the overdose. And as for praying, Job's knees are sore, his prayer book in tatters, and his searchlight stuck!

Introspection drives the sufferer deeper into despair, further tormenting one who needs to be freed from himself. It wears the rut into a grave. Like the death-track of one lost in a forest, introspection in times of desperation can keep one on an endless circle of self-deception.

The arrows
of the Almighty

Then Job answered: "O that my vexation
were weighed, and all my calamity laid in the
balances! For then it would be heavier than the
sand of the sea; therefore my words have been
rash. For the arrows of the Almighty are in me;
my spirit drinks their poison; the terrors of
God are arrayed against me. In truth I have
no help in me, and any resource is driven
from me" (6:1-4, 13).

Now Job voices his aloneness. This is the very pit of
pain. Each of us experiences it, as surely as life is ultimately "single file."

As infants in the doctor's office, what did we think
upon receiving that first shot? Surrounded by trusted
people, with mother protectively near, we must have
sensed, as the needle found its mark, that we were alone
in this experience. Even our very nearest were leagued
against us. This aloneness is what it means to be human.

In all mental and emotional stress, the seeming re-
moteness of trusted friends is frightening. But before Job
speaks of his friends, he pours forth his grievances against
God. He freely confesses that his words have been rash,
but he appeals to the right of the dying, the right to desperate overstatement.

Job's quarrel with God has the intensity of a lover's
quarrel. He addresses him whose existence he doesn't doubt,

but who appears to have turned against him. Like the words of lovers, Job's aren't prim or precise. His accusations aren't marshaled in orderly lines. They stumble over each other and rush like torrents from his full heart and frenzied mind.

From a friend

*"He who withholds kindness from a friend
forsakes the fear of the Almighty" (6:14).*

An alternate rendering of this passage, believed by
some to be more accurate, would say, "Mercy from his
friend is due to him that is in despair, even when he forsakes the fear of the Almighty" (Samuel Terrien, *Job:
Poet of Existence*, p. 56).

This is a bold thought, that true compassion cherishes
heretics even in their heresy. It places persons above their
beliefs. This is the key to preserving communication and
promoting healing in a pluralistic community. It encour-
ages full and honest expression by maintaining an un-
threatened and unthreatening mood of respect for all
people. But it is especially necessary in dealing with pain.

Job's friends come to him with a mold into which
they try to force him, and when he doesn't fit, they reject
him. They demonstrate that any orthodoxy lacking charity
is heresy, any doctrine inadequate for human extremity is
too narrow.

In defending God, Eliphaz has deserted Job. Twice he
has browbeaten Job with the finger-wagging word, "Behold!" Now Job pursues the sharp counterattack of one
who feels cornered and betrayed.

45

When it is hot

*"My brethren are treacherous as a torrent-bed;
as freshets that pass away, which are dark with
ice, and where the snow hides itself. In time of
heat they disappear; when it is hot, they vanish
from their place. The caravans turn aside from
their course; they go up into the waste, and
perish. The caravans of Tema look, the travelers
of Sheba hope. They are disappointed because
they were confident; they come hither and are
confounded. Such you have now become to
me"* (6:15-21a).

Job now speaks poignantly of his friends, how he has
looked to them in expectation and hope, only to be met
with judgment. He pictures the endangered traveler in
the hottest season of that desert land. What tragedy if a
caravan is invited to turn aside by one who recalls seeing a
watering place which no longer exists! How desperate the
situation if the remembered stream has become a dry river
bed!

They "look," they "hope," they are "disappointed"
and "confounded." Each of these words is charged with
pathos as Job describes his disillusionment with these
fair-weather friends.

At this point our memories lead us into troubled con-
templation of our failures and betrayals. The picture Job
paints haunts us, for we see in it our own faces; we con-

sider the shallowness of our commitments and the glibness of our promises to those who honor us with their trust. Long ago I asked a troubled young person if any one source of disillusionment stood out above all else. Immediately came the reply, "Christians, I guess!"

The titles we bear—"Christian," "friend"—raise high expectations which are often disappointed.

My world is crumbling

"Has not man a hard service upon the earth, and are not his days like the days of a hireling? Like a slave who longs for the shadow, and like a hireling who looks for his wages, so I am allotted months of emptiness, and nights of misery are apportioned to me. My days are swifter than a weaver's shuttle, and come to their end without hope. Therefore I will not restrain my mouth; I will speak in the anguish of my spirit; I will complain in the bitterness of my soul" (from 7:1-11).

Job's complaint against the Lord can be contained no longer. He is disillusioned with his existence. His bitterness spills over without control. Having experienced not only the devastation of property and person, but also the ensuing emotional and physical collapse, Job acts as if delirious, pitching and tossing in a fever of emptiness and meaninglessness.

Nights are long and mornings bring no relief. The cloud bank covers Job's entire sky. Time drags and flies simultaneously. He sees not only the heavy-footed side of hopelessness, but also its fleetness, as he fancies himself rushing toward oblivion. Under these conditions he abandons all discretion, accusing the Lord of sadistic tactics because he imprisons a person in life at the same time that he tortures him in every part. Job has become an exposed nerve.

Most of all, Job feels cornered by God, brought to a confused halt, forced to stand at bay under his all-seeing eye. Instead of rejoicing in God's attention, Job shrinks from God's apparent discrimination. He feels his sin rubbed in rather than blotted out.

What is man?

*"What is man, that thou dost make so much
of him, and that thou dost set thy mind upon
him, dost visit him every morning, and test
him every moment? How long wilt thou not
look away from me, nor let me alone till I
swallow my spittle?"* (7:17-19).

"What is man?" The psalmist has placed this question
into a framework of doxology and ecstatic praise: "When
I look at thy heavens, the work of thy fingers, the moon
and the stars which thou hast established; what is man
that thou art mindful of him, and the son of man that
thou dost care for him? Yet thou hast made him little
less than God, and dost crown him with glory and honor"
(Ps. 8:3-5).

Now Job turns this caring concern of God into the very
crux of his problem. He sees in God's unflagging attention
an unbearable oppression. Instead of rejoicing in humanity's special place, he cries out under the burden of it all
and shouts his rebellion against God's plan: "Why do
you make so much of me? You say you care for me. Well,
I can take better care of myself. Turn around, and give
me a little privacy!" This is the voice of one who feels
restrained and cramped in the caring love of God.

Here is a high point in the Book of Job. The God
who has called Job "my servant," who has spoken that
all-important word "mine," is the same God who has

loved all people into worth and worthiness. He has burdened us with the weight of a wonderful offering, his shaping and chastening love. He is not content to let us be who we are. He has great plans for us. But, like, Job, we are afraid to become what he wants us to be. It is inherent in our rebellion that we fear the best the most. Like Job, we would like to settle for less.

We find it awesome to live under the "my servant" claim of God; even as we pray "Thy will be done," we brace ourselves for the worst. We'd rather be left alone. It is difficult to let God be God.

You spy!

"If I sin, what do I do to thee, thou watcher of men? Why hast thou made me thy mark? Why have I become a burden to thee? Why dost thou not pardon my transgressions and take away my iniquity?" (7:20-21a).

Now Job, the trapped one, looks frantically for an exit. He wants out of this relationship which has become so threatening. He feels hunted, even haunted, by this man-watching God. He would like a lesser "peace." In the words of T. S. Eliot *(Murder in the Cathedral)*, "We fear the hand at the window, the fire in the thatch, the fist in the tavern, the push into the canal, less than we fear the love of God."

It is a classic motif in the history of the race, this search for exit, this strategy of escape. Ever since the fall, humans have tried to hide from God. We would like to redraft the plan, choose to be feline or bovine or canine rather than human.

Christian proclamation in worship gently but persistently blocks the exits we attempt to create in our religion, work, recreation, or whatever the preoccupation may be. We all hear the footfalls of the Hound of Heaven. In my own experience, whatever has profoundly shaken or reshaped me has been such that I should never have chosen it, if escape had been possible.

God does plague and irritate us. We want relief from

his kind of salvation. We prefer the spurious rest of spiritual coma to the restlessness of true discipleship. We prefer numbness to the pain of new concern and quest. God is a problem to us because he threatens those bondages which seem to be our very selves.

If you will seek God

Then Bildad the Shuhite answered: "How long will you say these things, and the words of your mouth be a great wind? Does God pervert justice? Or does the Almighty pervert the right? If your children have sinned against him, he has delivered them into the power of their transgression. If you will seek God and make supplication to the Almighty, if you are pure and upright, surely then he will rouse himself for you and reward you with a rightful habitation. And though your beginning was small, your latter days will be very great" *(8:1-7).*

Second in experience, position, and age, Bildad, too, tries to correct Job. Less tactful and perhaps even more frustrated than Eliphaz, he reiterates the doctrine of divine retribution, pressing deeper the dagger of suspicion.

Light turns to heat as Bildad talks down to Job and insultingly refers to Job's outcries as "a great wind." He even turns his accusations against Job's dead children as he stabs him with cruel "ifs." Job is indeed vulnerable, open to attack on many fronts, for he has loved much and had many to love. Bildad comes at him from the direction of his commitments as a father. It is easy to accuse the dead, for they offer no rebuttal. With a single

54

broadside blow, Bildad shifts the load of condemnation onto Job, the grieving father, by accusing his children.

Possibly Bildad intends a bit of kindness by pointing his finger in the direction of Job's children rather than directly at him, but he turns immediately from condolence to condemnation.

Consider the fathers

"For inquire, I pray you, of bygone ages, and
consider what the fathers have found" (8:8).

Stuck in the graveyard, Bildad uses the past wrongly.
He is shocked by Job's insinuation of divine injustice, and
he attempts to answer Job's rash words by appealing to
"the fathers." His catechism, like that of Eliphaz, is hard-
bound rather than loose-leaf, presenting a static point of
view. He is unwilling to join Job in his dynamic response
to suffering, his heroic struggle for new dimensions and
deeper meanings. He is afraid to be broken open to new
and more difficult questions or to reconsider great issues in
the fresh light of present experience. He is a reminder that
yesterday can become a prison if one forgets that God's
grace manifests itself as surprise and that the past must
never be the measure of the future.

Bildad oversimplifies Job's situation and uses the favorite tactic of the moralist, the rhetorical question. Throughout the exchange between Job and his three friends, the
real questions come from Job. The friends are not searching for answers.

Bildad's moralism seems designed to intimidate. The
pity is that today, too, one will find Bildad at the hospital
harassing the defenseless sufferer with nagging questions
and simplistic exhortations. The tragedy is that anything
so wrong can be made to appear so right. Uncle Bob
Bildad and Aunt Betty Bildad aim to set everyone straight.

They are loyal friends of the law, but no friends of either God or God's children.

If Eliphaz is the advisor, Bildad is the catechiser. He forgets there is a unique element in every new situation and resorts to platitudes as Band-Aids for Job's condition.

No umpire between us

Then Job answered: "Truly I know that it is
so: But how can a man be just before God? If
one wished to contend with him, one could not
answer him once in a thousand times. If it is a
contest of strength, behold him! If it is a matter
of justice, who can summon him? I loathe my
life. It is all one; therefore I say, he destroys
both the blameless and the wicked. My days are
swifter than a runner; they flee away, they see
no good. There is no umpire between us, who
might lay his hand upon us both" (from 9:1-35).

Job, usually thought of as one of the classic wrestlers
with God, now finds himself struggling also with the
work-righteous and self-centered stance into which both
Eliphaz and Bildad attempt to draw him. Already Job
shows signs of being influenced by their moralistic counsel, and he continues to move in that direction, deepening
his anguish of spirit.

Job now openly speaks of contending with God. He
feels caught in an unjust mismatch and is overwhelmed
by his sense of personal inadequacy. He laments the drain-
ing away of his strength and feels his life slipping into
the past. But even as hope grows dim, Job's asking is
deepened, and he rouses himself to express his most daring
desire, that there might be someone to stand between him
and the Lord.

"There is no umpire between us, who might lay his hand upon us both." This is the first of several expressions of longing for a mediator, someone to go between Job's delirious self and his silent God. Job's searchlight is trained on Bethlehem, sending its beam across the ages. His is the cry that no human can satisfy, the cry for the saving event.

I loathe my life

*"I loathe my life; I will give free utterance to
my complaint; I will speak in the bitterness of
my soul. I will say to God, Do not condemn
me; let me know why thou dost contend
against me. Thy hands fashioned and made me;
and now thou dost turn about and destroy me.
Remember that thou hast made me of clay; and
wilt thou turn me to dust again?"
(from 10:1-9).*

Job's agony spurs him to the boldness often possessed
by persons in pain. In the sickroom, masks fall off and
pretenses break down. It is no place for the easily offended. Supporting the sufferer requires great self-knowledge,
a shockproof, honest compassion, and acceptance.

Job now speaks out of the deepening bitterness in his
soul, oscillating between entreaty and complaint. He is a
strong swimmer in a turbulent sea, vacillating between
hopelessness and hope, at times submerged, then reappear-
ing to struggle on. He is plagued by the image of an angry
God, yet he never abandons belief in a living and loving
God. His creation by God's hand, normally a cause for
celebration, now becomes to Job a rankling torment. He
appeals to his Maker, "Remember that thou hast made me
of clay; and wilt thou turn me to dust again?"

Our faith, too, is checkered with doubt. Our praise
trails off into confession of weakness and weariness, and

"I believe" becomes "Help my unbelief!" We, like Job, are ambivalent in our thinking and praying—and especially in our feeling. While we may not, in our heart of hearts, believe ourselves to be forsaken, we fear such doom at times, only to come shuddering back to wavering hope.

Oh, that
God would speak!

Then Zophar the Naamathite answered:
"Should a multitude of words go unanswered,
and a man full of talk be vindicated? Should
your babble silence men, and when you mock,
shall no one shame you? For you say, 'My
doctrine is pure, and I am clean in God's eyes.'
But oh, that God would speak, and open his
lips to you, and that he would tell you the
secrets of wisdom! For he is manifold in under-
standing. Know then that God exacts of you
less than your guilt deserves" (11:1-6).

Enter Zophar in hobnailed boots. Cocksure and crude, uninhibited by courtesy or a reflective mind, he speaks as one who has never harbored a doubt. His heavy-footed judgment confirms that alienation which has prevailed since Eliphaz first addressed Job. Zophar's dogmatism allows for no margin of error and leaves him most poorly equipped to deal with one who is distraught. Angered by Job's many words and bold complaints, he rushes into the dangerous game of playing God.

Zophar seems to have a fine sense of the majesty and transcendent wisdom of God, but little sense of wonder with relation to God's dealings with his children. For Zophar everything is settled, so he is impatient with inquiry and discussion. He appears to have no respect for mystery, no experience of suffering.

Zophar is aroused. Innuendo and insinuation lurk in every word. He undermines Job with ifs and urges him to hypocritical self-abasement. He accuses Job of hiding something and resents the fact that he will not overconfess to please his judges. His cruelest blast is, in effect, "If I were God, you would be in a worse condition than you are!"

This encounter with Zophar doesn't advance the discussion but it points to the painful truth that, in a crisis, we tend to feel inadequate and so become angry. We grow fierce when we are afraid. The increasing cruelty of Job's counselors can be traced to the growing realization that their neat solutions and pat answers here are useless.

I am not
inferior to you

*Then Job answered: "No doubt you are the
people, and wisdom will die with you. But I
have understanding as well as you; I am not
inferior to you. Who does not know such
things as these?" (12:1-3).*

With a blast of sarcasm, Job brushes aside the ill-timed,
insensitive comments of his counselors. He says, in effect:
"Oh, yes, you are the people! You have a monopoly on
wisdom. You brought all knowledge with you, and when
you die you will take it with you." Not raw courage, but
inner integrity enables Job to stand alone against the
weight of popular opinion which these three represent.

Job stands off the siege in this spirited encounter by
charging Eliphaz, Bildad, and Zophar with brazen con-
ceit and arrogance. He tells them they are pretending to
be seers when they are really only sawing sawdust and
pushing tired thoughts around. In fact, they are trailing
behind Job. He needs fellowship to explore the new frontier of his present experience, help to press against the
unknown, and encouragement to rethink everything he has
hitherto believed and known. The three refuse to acknowledge the newness in the situation.

Job believes that "one with God is a majority." This
fortifies him in the coming test of endurance.

Later Job will again cry out, "Lo, my eye has seen
all this, my ear has heard and understood it. What you

know, I also know; I am not inferior to you" (13:1-2). But now the breakdown in communication results in reaction rather than response. From this point on, greater distance is created between Job and his counselors as the three talk past their suffering friend. The exchange becomes personal conflict—more heat and less light—with each side pressing its credentials.

As the dialog proceeds, Job's friends do not substantively advance the argument, but passion increases, especially Job's. Increasing alienation providentially turns Job more and more toward God. He appeals more and more desperately to his Creator, and cries for direct audience with him: "But I will speak to the Almighty, and I desire to argue my case with God. . . . Behold, he will slay me; I have no hope; yet I will defend my ways to his face. . . . Behold, I have prepared my case; I know that I shall be vindicated" (13:3, 15, 18).

Job is sure of himself, too sure, and later he will call back his words when God chastens him. Still, Job's inner integrity is impressive. He is willing to stand complete exposure and to let God "open the book."

Your own mouth condemns you

"Your own mouth condemns you, and not I;
your own lips testify against you" (15:6).

His dignity wounded, Eliphaz lashes out at Job in his second speech. Eliphaz is weighted with seniority and the prestige of his position. Job's words hurt him deeply. With undisguised anger he spews forth indignation on behalf of himself, his friends, and God. He is violently defensive, accusing Job of calling into question the competence and integrity of the three, and even the justice of God. He suggests that Job has trespassed on God by asking for audience with him, by wanting to justify himself in God's very presence.

The dialog is deteriorating, sinking more and more to the level of direct attack. In his second address, Bildad presses the theme of swift and certain destruction of the wicked, meaning Job: "Yea, the light of the wicked is put out, and the flame of his fire does not shine. The light is dark in his tent, and his lamp above him is put out. His strong steps are shortened and his own schemes throw him down. For he is cast into a net by his own feet, and he walks on a pitfall. A trap seizes him by the heel, a snare lays hold of him" (18:5-9).

Zophar, too, continues the offensive against Job: "Do you not know this from of old, since man was placed upon earth, that the exulting of the wicked is short, and the joy of the godless but for a moment? . . . This is the wicked man's portion from God, the heritage decreed for him by God" (20:4-5; 29).

Job's counselors feel resentment, but even deeper is their fear. Fear is often displayed by friends faced with insoluble problems and drawn into encounter with perennially painful questions. In *The Renewal of Man*, Alexander Miller commands our attention with these words:

> The really destructive atheism is not the denial of God, for that denial, if it is honest, keeps a man in the company of Job and other men of integrity. The really destructive atheism is fear of facts. For fear of facts, from whatever source they come, . . . is the existential denial that the world is God's and that, as the Letter to the Colossians puts it, "all things cohere in Christ."

Miserable comforters!

Then Job answered: "I have heard many such things; miserable comforters are you all. Shall windy words have an end? Or what provokes you that you answer? I also could speak as you do, if you were in my place; I could join words together against you, and shake my head at you. I could strengthen you with my mouth, and the solace of my lips would assuage your pain" (16:1-5).

Why does Job feel so cheated? Why this outburst of indignation? Probably because his friends have persisted in answering his questions of the heart with arguments of the mind, forgetting that it is futile to argue with feelings, since "the heart has reasons which reason does not know." Perhaps he feels that their talk has been too cheap, requiring nothing of them and giving nothing to him, for they have substituted debate for acts of love.

No one ever thinks his way out of despair. He must be rescued by the "event" of love. Explanations usually drive a despairing one deeper into lostness or prove to be untrue by pretending to be complete.

An arm on the shoulder, the gentle pressure of a warm and loving hand, a nod, a look, a smile, a kiss, sometimes a tear—these often provide all the language that one can endure. In these acts our words become flesh, and without these "events" we cannot sense the caring love of God.

Job's words, "miserable comforters are you all," can be a word of warning to us. Because discussion and spoken advice are less costly than action, we easily fall into the trap of paying lip service to love. Our words do become "windy" when unaccompanied by acts of mercy and understanding. Job's resentment—"I also could speak as you do, if I were in your place; I could join words together against you, and shake my head at you"—is readily understood by one who has been harshly judged when caught in the tendrils of inexplicable pain. There is nothing more exhausting to the sufferer than arid abstraction and labored effort at analysis and explanation.

"Love is a verb," says the banner in the fellowship hall, but these, too, can become windy words, cruel and taunting, if unaccompanied by acts of truth and justice. Love is, indeed, a verb. It is the costly word.

God has hated me

*"Surely now God has worn me out; he has
made desolate all my company. And he has
shriveled me up. He has torn me in his wrath,
and hated me; he has gnashed his teeth at me;
my adversary sharpens his eyes against me.
God gives me up to the ungodly, and casts
me into the hands of the wicked. I was at ease
and he broke me assunder; he seized me by the
neck and dashed me to pieces; he sets me up as
his target, his archers surround me. He slashes
upon my kidneys and does not spare; he pours
out my gall on the ground. He breaks me with
breach upon breach; he runs upon me like a
warrior"* (from 16:7-17).

This is perhaps the lowest point in the mountainous
terrain of the Book of Job. Here the suffering one bluntly
accuses God of being an active enemy. In dramatic detail
he pictures the Lord's attack.

I lived with this book for many years, believing that
this picture of the Enemy God was overdrawn and untrue
to the believer's experience. "It can't be as bad as that!"
I thought. The change came, for me, when my own 11-
year-old led me into the deep valley of her pain.

She had post-polio surgery involving muscle trans-
plants, radical incisions in the foot and leg. Pain was
intense, especially throughout the night following surgery.

I remember her mother and I standing at her bedside that morning, saddened by her drawn face and fevered lips—evidence of the anguish she had endured. My wife spoke to her comfortingly, "But you did pray, though, didn't you?" Looking almost defiantly at us, the child exclaimed, "Yes. But mother, last night, for a while it seemed like God was my enemy!"

Since then I have reflected that if a child can be required to endure such a fearful sense of abandonment, this experience cannot be far from any of us. And I must add that in the intervening years I, too, have looked into such an abyss of spiritual desolation.

It is best to be realistic about the blackouts and eclipses which can come without warning, even to those who have lived with God through the high places and low places of many years. We are indebted to all believers of every age who have survived the wild and lonely heights and valleys of desolation, and reported back to us that God is there.

Have pity!

"Know then that God has put me in the wrong, and closed his net about me. He has stripped from me my glory, and taken the crown from my head. He breaks me down on every side, and I am gone, and my hope has he pulled up like a tree. He has put my brethren far from me. My kinsfolk and my closest friends have failed me; the guests in my house have forgotten me; my maidservants count me a stranger. I am repulsive to my wife, loathsome to the sons of my own mother. Even young children despise me. All my intimate friends abhor me, and those whom I have loved have turned against me. Have pity on me, have pity on me, O you my friends, for the hand of God has touched me! (from 19:6-21).

Job's human world has become a wasteland, and those who might have affirmed him have become a horrifying *No!*

Brothers, acquaintances, kinsfolk, his own wife, little children, all those whom Job has loved—what a roll call of deserters! What a recital of broken promises! What a description of rejection! But who among us hasn't experienced some of this failure when called upon to demonstrate the courage and stamina of our love? We feel deep sympathy with "the paper Job," but in real life we are not there to be counted.

As if estrangement isn't enough, Job now suffers the humiliation of having become abhorrent. He who had attracted others is now repulsive even to his wife. Little children take their cue from adults and ridicule his helplessness. For a time he steeled himself against this onslaught of rejection, but now he cries out for pity.

But even as Job sees God's wrath in his present condition, he begins to turn more and more from those who have failed to affirm him to God himself, the only remaining *yes* in his crumbling world.

My Redeemer lives!

*"Oh that my words were written! Oh that they
were inscribed in a book! Oh that with an iron
pen and lead they were graven in the rock
forever! For I know that my Redeemer lives,
and at last he will stand upon the earth; and
after my skin has been thus destroyed, then
from my flesh I shall see God" (19:23-26).*

Here Job struggles with the hiddenness of God and his
deepest desire spills over—the desire for a "Goel," a vindicator, a redeemer who can bring justice by casting decisive
light on his case. Job knows that his appeal to posterity
is insufficient, but he nevertheless expresses the wish that
his record might be given permanence so that those who
come after him may be finally assured of his innocence.
Only the "iron pen and lead" will be sufficient for such a
record, and he wants it to be engraved in something hard,
like rock, lest it be lost.

The reference to the redeemer, the "Goel" of ancient
times, concerns the responsibility of the "next of kin" to
a deceased relative, spelled out in ancient law and exem-
plified in the relationship of Boaz to Ruth (Ruth 2–4).
However, in the course of Christian events the Church has
turned Job's sigh into its song. While there is danger in
pushing these words of Job too far, there is also danger in
throttling them too much. We can't verbalize Job's dream
or desire but we do recognize that Job lives in the head-

lines of the spiritual history of our race, and therefore we sing Job's words with Christ's meaning.

As Christians, saved by grace through faith in Christ, we make our home in his alien righteousness, glorying in his cross and resurrection, receiving him as our Savior and Redeemer. This righteousness is alien in the sense that it is entirely beyond and outside of us. We can do nothing to merit it; it can only be ours by gift. The Christ who is God's kept promise to every sinner is also our faith's vindicator and our eternal Lord.

Why do the wicked grow mighty?

"Why do the wicked live, reach old age, and grow mighty in power? Their children are established in their presence, and their offspring before their eyes. Their houses are safe from fear, and no rod of God is upon them. Their bull breeds without fail; their cow calves, and does not cast her calf. They send forth their little ones like a flock, and their children dance. They sing to the tambourine and the lyre, and rejoice to the sound of the pipe. They spend their days in prosperity, and in peace they go down to Sheol. They say to God, 'Depart from us! We do not desire the knowledge of thy ways. What is the Almighty, that we should serve him? And what profit do we get if we pray to him? (21:7-15).

I remember as a child eating my favorite pie with tears running down my cheeks. I might as well have been eating chalk, for I was examining everyone else's plate for "justice" and thought that I'd been cheated. My mistake was in looking around instead of up, for a thankful heart would have provided all the flavor I was missing. I'm sure now that I'd been lovingly and fairly dealt with, but envy can poison the sweetest situation.

Job is also poisoning himself by looking around, but he is looking out of suffering, not at the good and just, but at the crooked and uncaring. Many such people with high visibility today, have cheated their way to the top and crushed others in the process. No level of pain in the Book of Job is easier for us to identify with than Job's envy of the spectacular success of cruel people. Many are our moments of bitter resentment as we watch their swift rise to prominence and power, their flaunting of their best-selling autobiographies. We, like Job, have cried for justice!

We can only bow our heads if we state the case against Job. His complaint against God is both presumptuous and rash, but who among us can cast the first stone?

Job's perspective is too limited to allow him to pass judgment on God or to correct the Almighty. God will check him. God loves Job too much to let him destroy himself in this way. There will be an accounting and Job will be surprised.

God pays no attention

"Why are not times of judgment kept by the Almighty, and why do those who know him never see his days? Men remove landmarks; they seize flocks and pasture them. They drive away the ass of the fatherless; they take the widow's ox for a pledge. They thrust the poor off the road; the poor of the earth all hide themselves. . . . From out of the city the dying groan, and the soul of the wounded cries for help; yet God pays no attention to their prayer" (24:1-4, 12).

Like a page from this morning's newspaper, this ancient picture of wickedness unfolds before us. It reminds us that, though love is infinitely various and incessantly creative, hatred and evil are utterly lacking in originality. People of our day do, indeed, "thrust the poor off the road." The weak go to the wall while the strong exploit and vandalize with all their power and cunning. The "fatherless," the unprotected, are dehumanized and banished to their ghettos, captives in their own land.

In appointing himself attorney for the defense of the defenseless, Job presses his case against God with eloquence and power. He not only complains; he accuses. Earlier Job has seen God as enemy. Now he sees him as the great void. He rails against legalized murder and robbery, which are rampant in his society, and against dis-

78

respect for law and disregard for humane practices. He is tired of waiting for a God who isn't at home, a God who wraps himself in silence in the midst of the cries of his children. He is angered by the secret that becomes a wall between God and the sufferer: "Why do those who know him never see his day?"

We are all too familiar with the experience of waiting. With the psalmists we have raised the frantic and angry cry, "How long?" The quiet strength of endurance relies on a maturity we don't possess.

Nothing less than presence—loving, speaking, revealing —nothing less than the God who offers himself as solace and salvation can suffice for Job. And when will he respond? The Voice, the Voice from anywhere—may it even be from the whirlwind?—is Job's need. The story runs on. But Job the attorney is also the sufferer, waiting on the Lord.

Failure to embrace

And Job again took up his discourse, and said . . . (27:1).

The words of Eliphaz, Bildad, and Zophar are ended. We have come to a series of independent discourses by Job. But first let us ask, Where did the three friends fail? What opportunities did they miss? What might they have been to Job?

Clearly, they failed to *embrace* Job. Overwhelmed by mystery and incongruity, Job clamored for explanations no one can command. But beyond his need for rational solutions lay the deeper longing to be cherished. Job needed to be affirmed by a community embrace. He needed someone to be there. God's presence is mediated through persons who are truly present, actively and lovingly listening to the lonely one.

A friend recounted to me one of his face-to-the-wall moments. In the space of a few months, he had suffered a series of heart attacks, one of them severe. In this period he had also experienced the death of his beloved wife. So overwhelming was his grief that he literally turned his face to the wall, inconsolable and despairing. Friends came, with their best thoughts and prayers, but the shadows did not lift. He lay day after day, not caring whether people came or what they said.

One morning he sensed that someone was standing at the threshold of his hospital room. It proved to be an aged pastor. Slowly he came round the bed. Then he bent low, so low that for a brief moment his cheek touched that of the despairing one. He softly said, "The Lord will take care of you, my son!" Then he left. This became the Great Divide, the turnabout moment. From then on his convalescence was steady.

Not many words, not clever or new, but they were accompanied by touch and they conveyed embrace. Recalling words, words from home, reminding words— plain, clear, and healing.

The one who comes in love is a letter from home, a living epistle which cannot fail. Love's successes are sometimes between the lines. When we feel like running away for lack of readiness, lack of words, when we look for somebody else to comfort the sufferer, we need to be reminded that the main thing is to be present.

The Spirit works through person and presence. Give him an instrument; he will play. Offer yourself to be used. He will do the rest.

Failure to dare

And Job again took up his discourse, and said . . . (27:1).

The failure to receive and embrace a sufferer isn't rooted only in lack of compassion; it is as often failure in courage. Early in the encounter, Job accused his counselors, "You see my calamity and are afraid" (6:21b). Their actions betray their dread of involvement in the struggle Job is enduring. They glimpse the mystery and falter; they look over the edge and draw back.

In fear of knowing others, we betray fear of knowing ourselves. In closing our hearts to the despair of another, we avoid honest confrontation with our own beings. No courage brings greater rewards than the courage to accompany a struggling one beyond one's own depth and to face with the sufferer the mystery of one's own being. In sharing another's despair, we receive more help than we can give.

Recalling many of my failures, I must confess: I didn't dare to be as impulsive as I was called to be. I didn't dare to do love's unconventional bidding. I was afraid to break out of the proper line, to speak the improper word, to show love where the situation required it. I hesitated to be a "little Christ" to the one in need.

It is too late to retrace my steps and minister to those who have needed me. By refusing to join them in grappling with suffering, I left part of my life unlived. The sadness with which I sometimes thumb the calendar can be traced to this failure in courage. Cowardice too often prevented me from redeeming the time.

Job's friends failed to dare. Their failure speaks its message to each of us. God waits for us to take Christ's incarnation seriously by becoming involved with people. We are called to break the silence concerning God's love, so that, in us, the good word of love becomes flesh. We don't need to be afraid of "nothing to say" in critical situtions. The need isn't for clever conversationalists. Loving silence makes a powerful sound. One doesn't always need answers for questions spilling over out of the delirium of grief, but one does need companions in the quest.

Suffering is not peripheral but central to human existence. To avoid situations of pain is to condemn oneself to the shallows of life. Wherever we are called to be, there God is already present. He goes before us, still calling, "Follow me."

Failure to bend

And Job again took up his discourse, and said . . . (27:1).

Closely related to failure to dare is failure, or refusal, to bend. Job's friends are too rigid to make the creative response which suffering demands. They try to force Job into their narrow theological box. Their arguments are well stated, but less than life-size. Their dogma fails to take into account Job's suffering. To defend their position, they are forced to oversimplify. Life's ultimate questions always remain, while the answers are transitory. A life too full of answers has usually been trivialized.

Claiming full and final answers is perilous because it forces one to pretend to an unreal degree of comprehension. God's ways with his children lead into profound mysteries and involve us in ultimate issues. If we seek simple explanations of life's mysteries, we remake the Giver of life in our own image and scale down our faith to the degree that it no longer supports life.

Significance is found on the far side of loneliness. The crowds milling around bargain counters have little thought for the pearl of great price. It is best to march to the beat of a distant drum.

Defensiveness is the posture of the weak and uncertain. Job needed bold pioneers; instead he got stolid settlers. To his friends he appeared to be a menace to society, a threat to familiar faith.

We can't befriend others when we must defend ourselves. Moats and fortresses don't permit forward march. Insecurities are enemies of open communication and true community. The witch-hunt has always been the coward's game. The weak persecute while the strong listen—and are changed.

But where shall wisdom be found?

"But where can wisdom be found? And where is the place of understanding? Man does not know the way to it, and it is not found in the land of the living. The deep says, 'It is not in me,' and the sea says, 'It is not with me.' It cannot be gotten for gold, and silver cannot be weighed as its price. God understands the way to it, and he knows its place. For he looks to the ends of the earth, and sees everything under the heavens. And he said to man, 'Behold, the fear of the Lord, this is wisdom; and to depart from evil is understanding'" (from 28:12-28).

Argument and passion are now laid aside as the inspired poet brings us the celebrated hymn to wisdom. Contrasting wisdom with all that can be purchased in the marketplace, he praises it as the possession solely of the Creator. No creature should aspire to be its claimant. For human beings, wisdom is fear of the Lord.

Faith's affirmation, its commitment to the unseen and incomprehensible, is the leap that is required. The wisdom which we, together with Job, so much desire is beyond our reach. We must stake our lives on the faith that God will be true, and trust in his goodness and justice. Worship and trust befit one who would be counted wise.

This discourse has been called a "musical interlude," separating the debate from Job's final soliloquy. It shows how far Job has forged ahead of his friends. He has become their counselor. His stature is vastly greater than theirs. He hasn't overcome their intractability, their passion for pat answers, but his own vision has broadened and deepened. He has risen to heights of insight hitherto unknown to him or to his would-be mentors.

When God was with me

*"Oh, that I were as in the months of old, as in
the days when God watched over me; when his
lamp shone upon my head, and by his light I
walked through darkness; as I was in my
autumn days, when the friendship of God was
on my tent; when the Almighty was yet with
me, when my children were about me. I put on
righteousness, and it clothed me; my justice
was like a robe and a turban. I was eyes to the
blind, and feet to the lame"* (29:1-5, 14-15).

Job's faith has slipped into the past tense. He can't
praise; he can only lament. But his lament takes the form
of a self-portrait, a picture of the compassionate leader
whom he sees himself to have been, a picture of classic
beauty and completeness. Job eulogizes himself and pines
for the vanished glory of his autumn days, the fruitful
period of his life.

When his children played at his feet and his abundance
increased daily, when his universal acceptance brought
him unbounded respect and adulation, "those were the
days." His mere presence silenced young and old alike.
Even royalty deferred to him. He championed the weak
and leaped to the stranger's defense. Oppressors feared
him and the dying blessed him. He was "eyes to the blind"
and dwelt "like a king among his troops."

But all this is to buttress Job's accusation against the

injustice of the God who has forsaken him. Goaded by his long siege and the stubborn hiddenness of the God whom he longs to address face to face, Job overdraws his self-portrait, slipping into illusion. He needs to be lifted out of his self-concentration and swept into the vast orbit of God's purpose for all people and God's dream for him.

Like a prince

*"If I have walked with falsehood, and my foot
has hastened to deceit; (Let me be weighed in a
just balance, and let God know my integrity!)
Oh, that I had one to hear me! (Here is my
signature! let the Almighty answer me!) Oh,
that I had the indictment written by my adversary! Surely I would carry it on my shoulder;
I would bind it on me as a crown; I would give
him an account of all my steps; like a prince I
would approach him"* (31:5-6, 35-37).

Goaded by the siege of his accusing friends and exas-
perated by God's long silence, Job now hurls his challenge to God and men to prove him guilty of any wrong.
He cries out his readiness to sign a plea of innocence and
pit it against any and every indictment in heaven or on
earth.

Job now pictures himself as "prince," laden with
medals, erect and confident, facing God with regal bearing,
never flinching before his eyes. Job forgets the complaints
he has lodged against God and his spoken rebellion, re-
membering only his splendid career among his peers. He
speaks rash words, words of defiant pride, words which
will haunt him in the moment of truth and cause him to
lay his hand upon his mouth.

We see both the grandeur and the misery of this great
man in his moment of self-deception, and we cannot but

admire one so noble, even as we tremble for his pride. We sense that he is trespassing and we cringe. It is easy for us to stand aloof and "rend our garments" as Job speaks of wearing the crown, but we are no strangers to the language of pride. Indeed, this finds us where we live and exposes our boastings for what they are.

Let thorns grow

*"If I have walked with falsehood, if my heart
has been enticed to a woman, if I have rejected
the cause of my manservant or my maidservant,
if I have withheld anything that the poor
desired, if I have seen anyone perish for lack of
clothing, if I have made gold my trust, if I
have rejoiced in the ruin of him that hated me,
if I have concealed my transgressions from men,
if my land has cried out against me, and its
furrows have wept together; if I have eaten its
yield without payment, and caused the death of
its owners; let thorns grow instead of wheat,
and foul weeds instead of barley" (from
31:5-40).*

This is clearly the language of oath, generally referred
to as Job's oath of clearance. For us it etches the ethical
outline of Job's life with others, expressing his values as
clansman and farmer, a picture of integrity in the context
of his culture. One could almost call it a dramatization of
the Decalog.

But it is more. It is Job's presentation of his case, his
claim of merit and his denial of guilt before both God
and men. It is his answer to every indictment that can be
brought against him. By implication it is a boast, and,
as such, a precarious statement, even as it eloquently describes Job's humane commitments.

Then Elihu
became angry

Then Elihu the son of Barachel the Buzite,
of the family of Ram, became angry (32:2).

We have repeatedly spoken of three counselors, but there is a fourth, the angry intruder, Elihu. Now, with an egotistical fanfare, he makes his dramatic entrance.

Scholarly research has led many to conclude that this portion of the book is a later addition. Some maintain that it contributes nothing to the book. It is our contention that Elihu does further the discussion and provide a new emphasis.

Elihu has loitered impatiently at the edge of the circle, listening with increasing disgust and growing more and more eager to have his say. Because of his youth, he says, he has waited for experience to speak, but he feels that he has waited in vain. He has sided with the counselors against Job, and he believes their case against Job is right. But he is also angry with the three because he believes they have stated their case inadequately. He is furious with them because they have not silenced Job.

Elihu impresses with his brash confidence. "I" and "me" and "my" dominate the early portion of his discussion, appearing more than 50 times in his long introduction and his first address (Chapters 32 and 33). He speaks down to all of them, claiming wisdom by inspired visions and a fullness which has brought him to the bursting point.

God opens
the ears of men

"You say, 'I am clean, without transgression;
I am pure, and there is no iniquity in me.'
Behold, in this you are not right. I will answer
you. God is greater than man. Why do you
contend against him, saying, 'He will answer
none of my words'? For God speaks in one way,
and in two, though man does not perceive it.
In a dream, in a vision of the night, when deep
sleep falls upon men, while they slumber in
their beds, then he opens the ears of men, and
terrifies them with warnings, that he may turn
man aside from his deed, and cut off pride from
man; he keeps back his soul from the Pit, his
life from perishing by the sword" (from
33:9-18).

Job has charged God with paying no attention to him.
"Oh, that God would speak!" Elihu contends that God
speaks in many ways. Accusing Job of pride, Elihu says
God has spoken many times to warn of impending dis-
aster, lest Job be totally destroyed by his sin.

Job's discussion with the three focused almost exclu-
sively on God's justice in punishing Job and on the neces-
sity of Job making full confession of hidden sins. Elihu
contends that suffering provides a stoplight in the path
to destruction, that it is intended to rescue Job from
himself.

94

It is true that pride lures us all, inviting us to try to play God, but it tempts especially the rich and the powerful. It is also true that the one thing worse than sin accompanied by suffering would be sin without suffering. As Robert Frost has so charmingly pointed out, if we never found a tree across the road we would never stop to ask ourselves who we think we are. Highway signs must give way to danger signals when the road is washed out.

Elihu also points to God's grace and goodness in the midst of chastening the sinner: "Behold, God does all these things twice, three times, with a man, to bring back his soul from the Pit, that he may see the light of life" (33:29-30).

Then!

*Then the Lord answered Job
out of the whirlwind (38:1).*

One word stops us, like a traffic officer's upraised hand.
The single word *then* provides a bridge suggesting movement and purpose. All that has happened is prelude and
preparation; now comes the main event.

In the creation story (Genesis 1) this word signals the
climactic happenings: "Then God said, 'Let us make man
in our image.' " In the unfolding of the drama of redemp-
tion, God's *then* is expressed as fullness of time: "But in
the fullness of time God sent forth his son."

Time always flows toward fullness. It is alive with
God's purpose. He is at work even when we are tear-
blinded by pain and tested by sudden blackouts. Everything ticks if only we hear it. But God's *then* isn't ours.
We often feel, as Job did, that God's clock has stopped
and he will never show his face again.

"Then the Lord answered." This is the moment of
breakthrough for Job, the moment that had to come
though Job despaired of its arrival. Many of us have felt
at times like giving up on God, when sheer eyestrain has
forced us to stop looking for him, or so we thought. But
perhaps God knows that we haven't stopped looking, even
when we think we have. Perhaps he reads desires and
longings, even when they are buried beneath cries and
curses hurled into the heavens.

The fact

Then the Lord answered Job (38:1).

The search for a key to the complexities of this book ends here. In this unobtrusive line, easily lost as one reads, lies the key unlocking the central significance of the Book of Job, letting in God's revelatory light.

Not what God said, but the fact that he answered, is our first consideration. In this event we encounter the good news of the God who is always present, who bends his ear in response to the cry of his child. Here we pick up the motif of both the Old and New Testaments: the Lord sees, he hears, he cares. A good friend of mine illustrates this with the following story.

A young soldier-son hasn't written home for many months. His mother waits eagerly for some word as she unfailingly writes the family news and assures him of their love. She even sends an occasional gift to keep home in his heart. Still no word comes. Then one day this letter arrives: "Dear Mom, It's been a long time since I've written but everything is going OK. The women here wash their clothes down at the seashore. The men mostly fish. Hope you are all OK. I am. So long for this time. Bill."

That is all, but the mother is ecstatic. She proudly tells her friends that she received a letter from Bill. Only a crumb for her hunger, a shamefully meager response to all that she has done, but a response, nevertheless, and this is what she has longed for.

Response. In the fullness of time, God responded abundantly to his lost world. In this fact we see the Christ-face of reality. We relight our burned-out lamps by the light of the Star, the Risen One, and hope is reborn in the night.

The grace moment

Then the Lord answered Job (38:1).

We find it hard to leave this verse, and we do well to stay awhile, for it brings much for the heart to feed on.

This is the point at which grace penetrates the human situation, effecting the decisive turnabout in the case of Job. Here is the invasion from beyond all human resources, the act of saving rescue.

Job has nothing left. Possessions, position, person, family, community—everything and everyone are lost. All except God, the one who has called him "my servant." And now Job receives his answer.

Human bankruptcy is no news. Human lostness is just the dreariest of truths. This great book has seemed to break down like a massive truck, miring itself into mud. The middle chapters express sputtering helplessness, both of the counselors and of the sufferer himself. These men have reached the dead end of their thinking and explaining. Just the crumpling of a much crumpled thing, such is the book until this verse, "Then the Lord answered Job."

Have you ever received news so distressing it seemed to choke you and you had to swallow hard just to get your breath? Have you waited through a long night for a second word, which, when it came, was worse than the first? Have you lived with a burden so great that even the passing time could promise no release, for there wasn't that much future? If you have, you are prepared to hear the music in the word *then*. This is the good news, that the Lord has been with Job all the time. And he isn't only there, but also here in the aching present, nearer than breathing, closer than hands and feet.

The God who listens

Then the Lord answered Job (38:1).

To know God as listener is to know him as father. All personal relationship begins and continues in response. People shrivel into nothing with no one to listen to them. Human derelicts of every type reach out in desperate search for those who hear, spilling out their pathetic, pleading questions. The classic pathos of our age is that we fail to hear one another.

No one but God could satisfy Job, whose hunger was deeper than he knew. What Job didn't know about himself, the Lord knew. And today, too, our God runs ahead of our prayers. He answers beyond our capacity to ask. He leads us to the right questions.

Job's questions, though inadequate, reflect the turmoil of an honest heart. Not patience, but honesty is the mark of distinction in this, God's servant. In this honesty the Lord now finds his opportunity.

Who is this?

"Who is this that darkens counsel
by words without knowledge?" (38:2).

Here it is, the Lord's question, clearing the field and sending all human questions scurrying for cover. The Lord's question undresses each of us and shames our smaller inquiries.

Job not only has questions; he has become a question. To his friends he is a massive roadblock to simplistic orthodoxy, a shaker of foundations, a threat to security. To himself he is an unbearable burden. But always and forever, to the Lord he is "my servant," the battered child needing healing embrace.

The Lord's question isn't "What are you saying, Job?" but "Who are you? Whose child? Whose creation?" The Lord moves past the man's questions to get to the man. He cuts through the intellectual underbrush to expose the total person. Job's questions are important, but not as important as Job. Job thought his first need was for answers, but his first need is for the Answerer. Person hungers for Person.

Salvation isn't information, but rescue liberation. God reveals himself, not to explain, but to accomplish his purpose. That purpose is to take each of our lives into his own, that we may be re-created and reborn. The speaker is of prior importance to what is said.

Job has forgotten who he is. In his desperation he

speaks presumptuously and arrogantly. Now God holds the mirror before Job's face with the question, "Who is this?"

In the words of Samuel Terrien: "Now at last God himself speaks. He does not accuse Job of ethical transgression, but reveals to him by ironical questioning that man has no right to judge the Deity because man cannot conceive the Deity except in terms of some human image. God's wisdom and power are truly beyond man's grasp, and man may not trespass beyond the bounds of his humanity" (Interpreter's Bible, Vol. 3, p. 1170).

Words
without knowledge

"Who is this that darkens counsel
by words without knowledge?" (38:2).

The Lord's first word to Job is indeed a humbling one. Job's many words have exposed his inadequate perspective. His judgment against God is nothing less than a judgment of the finite upon infinitude.

Now the Lord says, in effect, "Who is this who questions me, this pretender who adds misery to misery by playing God? Who is this who calls my order disorder and says, 'It's all a mess!'"

Even as we note the Lord's catechization of Job we must also recognize that the God of the Book of Job is peculiarly the God who lets himself be asked. God is not threatened by the freedom of his child. Job wildly misuses his freedom, resorting to effrontery, blasphemy, and raging. While the Lord gives Job his rein, he summarily refuses the petty and pompous half-truths of his would-be defenders.

God doesn't let himself become trapped into argument, however "good" that argument may be. He simply shows himself. He is the God beyond the last counselor. We cannot reach him through the last door at the psychiatric clinic, but he reaches us through that first and last door, Jesus Christ, his Son!

I-Thou

"Gird up your loins like a man, I will question you, and you shall declare to me" (38:3).

The Lord of the whirlwind doesn't explain or apologize. He doesn't placate or patronize. And he won't be accused or catechized. He seeks no self-justification. He is the Lord!

"Gird up your loins. Get ready, Job. The moment you've demanded has come. Who are you to judge or to take my place?"

Here Person encounters person. Human beings have the capacity for "with-ness"; a person can never be an it. To stand in I-Thou relationship with the Lord is to live in the painful glory of divine address. It is to be held responsible and called to account, even for "every idle word."

In this divine-human meeting, Job is the Lord's concern, and back of his judgment is love. But even as we know that Love is on the march, we find this book dangerous and sobering, a judgment on our craving for the trivial and immediate. Its message defies all cheap and easy God-talk, and its implications are disquieting, even terrifying.

Where were you?

*"Where were you when I laid the foundation
of the earth? Tell me, if you have understanding. Who determined its measurements—
surely you know!" (38:4-5).*

"Whose dream, Job? And who brought it into being?
Who laid the foundations of all that is? Not you, Job,
and not you and I. I—only I!"

Job has pressed his grievances against the Lord. He has
charged him with indifference and hostility. Now the
Lord lets him feel the first tremors of the spiritual earth-
quake about to occur.

The Lord begins by reminding Job of his inadequate
perspective as a creature who "was not there," one who
can't know the beginning or the end. Job's screen is too
small for him to assess all that must be known to govern
the universe. Yet, with this limited understanding, he has
turned faultfinder and clamored for the moment of truth.

That moment has arrived. Job is about to learn that life
—his life—isn't a man-sized gift. It is not of human
invention. It is God's dream and he alone can be trusted
to fulfill it. In this trust Job will again find health.

The morning song

". . . when the morning stars sang together, and
all the sons of God shouted for joy" (38:7).

The language and mood are those of the poet, for creation calls for cosmic celebration. The story of creation is
the story of a divine frolic, the Father preparing a treasure
hunt for his children. He shows his love toward all that
he creates and anticipates.

Creation is a cathedral event. It calls for candles. Its
mystery defies investigation and invites celebration.

In unsurpassed beauty of thought and language, the
Book of Job here invites us to lose ourselves in praise of
the Creator, whose every *what* counters every *why*. It
invites us to raise questions of meaning and purpose, religious questions.

Inquiry on any level is not disparaged. But the hungers
of the heart outrun the reaches of the mind. These words
say to every modern Job: Ask, search, explore! And, in
all your asking, hear the singing of the morning stars.

Declare, if you know

"Have you commanded the morning since your days began, and caused the dawn to know its place? Have you entered into the springs of the sea, or walked in the recesses of the deep? Have the gates of death been revealed to you, or have the gates of deep darkness? Have you comprehended the expanse of the earth? Declare, if you know all this" (38:12, 16-18).

Now Job is asked to listen to the wordless eloquence of the created universe and to hear its secrets named but not exposed. He is caused to sense mystery in the good, even as he struggles with mystery in pain and evil. The mysteries of the creation and preservation of the universe are brought before Job. God reminds him that the march of time, with each unrepeatable dawn, is ever new and always different. It is almost as though the Lord were saying, "Job, how about your taking charge of just one sunrise or creating one drop of dew? I'll take care of all the rest!"

Each mystery touches the edge of a larger mystery and each successive depth leads to increasing gravity. Job's very creatureliness is pressed upon him, to rob him of words and to help him hear the Lord. The mouth is stopped to unstop the ear. Dumb wonder is to pass into new insight and attention.

"Have the gates of death been revealed to you?" The secret of secrets is death. Human pride finds no food here. Arrogance has nothing to live on. Ignorance of death is the fullest evidence of every mortal's need. This is the ultimate witness to Job's helplessness.

Surely you know

*"You know, for you were born then, and
the number of your days is great" (38:21).*

Three times the Lord ruffles Job's hair with the embarrassing word *know*. With gentle—or not so gentle—humor, Job is reminded of his accusations and what they implied. Few days and limited knowledge, nursery experience and kindergarten competence—all of these reminders are pressed upon Job to turn the man into a child.

This is not Job, the laughingstock of his former friends, destroyed and downgraded by foul-weather deserters. This is rather the beloved child, affectionately rebuked for his pretensions so he might find health again. Job needs more than to be held. He needs strong medicine, wisely administered. Therefore, the Lord parades his glory before him, not to blind but to heal him. He offers the balm of his presence and the caress of his hand.

God's storehouses

*"Have you entered the storehouses of the snow,
or have you seen the storehouses of the hail?"
(38:22).*

"Job, I am the living God. My purpose is to create and sustain life. Life is my gift to all living things. Therefore I cherish and provide for it. I protect this gift above all else."

Perhaps this is what the Lord is saying in the lengthy review of what we call weather. Can it be that there are profound religious implications in the daily weather report, meanings we miss?

Snow, hail, east wind, rain, thunder, dew, ice, lightning, mist—all of these and more are reviewed in the context of Job's arrest at the hand of the whirlwind Lord. Don't these phenomena manifest the flow of change, the continuing God-event of preservation and providence? Don't they reflect the ongoing activities of God as he sustains the many rhythms necessary to all that lives? Isn't this God's way of governing, shaping, controlling, and guiding all he has made? Surely our reflections on these delicate balances and counterbalances cause all of us —every contemporary Job—to sense the absolute dependence upon God which is our essential condition.

Where no man is

*"Who has cleft a channel for the torrents of
rain, and a way for the thunderbolt, to bring
rain on a land where no man is, on the desert in
which there is no man, to satisfy the waste and
desolate land, and to make the ground put forth
grass?" (38:25-27).*

As a very young child, my greatest fear was of darkness.
At times it even kept me awake. My father's study was
just across the hall, where often he would be at work at
my bedtime. In a moment of panic I would cry out,
frantic for a response. And the response always came:
"Go to sleep, I'm right here!" With this assurance I would
rest.

My father didn't bring a light—I would have liked that
—but he gave me something better, the assurance of his
loving presence. A light would have left me alone. In real
need, it couldn't satisfy. Presence, loving presence, is what
I craved.

Job would have liked a light in his darkness, a ready
answer to his terrifying questions. Instead he is given
caring Presence. Baffling as the barrage of unanswerables
must have been, he couldn't fail to get the larger message,
"I'm right here!"

"I'm right here, Job, rejoicing in my creation, loving
every part of it, except its pain. I'm in its struggles, Job,
even the struggle of the desert flower that grows in that

112

cracked rock. I love the lone, scraggy tree that bends with the wind. I care for each blade of grass. And I care for you, Job, especially in your need.

"I walk in the wastelands, for I made them. Vastness doesn't mean abandonment. I'm right here in this 'forsaken place,' and I'm with you."

The Lord reminds Job of his love-pledge even to the unpeopled wastelands, offering this as a double guarantee to Job, his costlier creature. Here the Lord's voice from the whirlwind calls across the centuries and blends with the voice of the Lord Christ: "If God so clothes the grass of the field, which today is alive and tomorrow is thrown into the oven, will he not much more clothe you, O men of little faith?" (Matt. 6:30).

Can you, Job?

*"Can you bind the chains of the Pleiades, or
loose the cords of Orion? Can you lead forth
the Mazzaroth in their season? Who can
number the clouds by wisdom? Or who can tilt
the waterskins of the heavens, when the dust
runs into a mass and the clods cleave fast
together?" (from 38:31-38).*

Job has been burdened by rank and position. He has
been accustomed to command. Now the Lord, who has
given him a sweeping look at a few of the numberless
mysteries around him, asks him to look up to the heavens.
He deluges him with questions, reminding him of his
limited authority and understanding: Can you bind the
chains of the Pleiades? Can you lead forth the Mazzaroth?
Do you know the ordinances of the heavens? Can you send
forth lightnings? Each question demonstrates the puniness
of Job's human energies.

Then abruptly the questions shift from Job, who *cannot*, to the Lord, who *can*: Who can number the clouds?
Who can tilt the waterskins of the heavens?

All the beauty and order in nature, so visible and yet so
mysterious, should remind Job and us that we are blessed
far beyond our capacity to comprehend. Both love and
authority lie in the Creator's hand. This is the moral
order which Job has rashly questioned and presumed to
judge.

114

Who provides?

"Can you hunt the prey for the lion, or satisfy the appetite of the young lions? Who provides for the raven its prey? Do you know when the mountain goats bring forth? Is it by your wisdom that the hawk soars and spreads his wings toward the south?" (from 38:39—39:26)

The questions tumble over each other, submerging and silencing Job, ranging now through the world of animate creatures. The voice from the whirlwind proclaims that all living things live with their faces toward God. The guiding instincts by which they order their existence are divinely implanted. The inner structures of life on every level are his.

All life is interconnected and points to the Lord, who is its source. Again, the inspired poet of Job suggests a flight to the words of Christ: "Are not two sparrows sold for a penny? And not one of them will fall to the ground without your Father's will" (Matt. 10:29). All that inhabit the jungles, climb the mountains, roam the desert plains, or soar in the open skies are bound to the Lord's loving hand. He broods over everything he has made.

Job is reminded that he doesn't understand what is beneath him and around him. How much less can he expect to see through the secrets of himself and of his Lord! How unequipped is he to judge!

He who argues with God

*And the Lord said to Job: "Shall a faultfinder
contend with the Almighty? He who argues
with God, let him answer it" (40:1-2).*

Job has clamored and complained. He has stood tall.
God would have him stand taller by bending low.

Job has been wise, but God would make him wiser.
Job has underestimated himself, as we all do whenever we
bring grievances against God. Pride isn't overestimation.
If we know we are God's children, we will think, not less,
but more of ourselves and the God who created us.

Before God, we are always in the wrong. Litany is our
fitting language. Like Job, we haven't respected the throne.
We have toyed with truth and tried to snatch the crown.
Our complaints bear witness against us.

It seems cruel that in the midst of so much misery, Job
is cut back and further tormented. But he has wanted to
play God. He has trespassed; he can't be healed without
hurt. Perhaps this is the meaning of God's relentless chastening. The Gardener prunes the branches, sometimes
cutting most deeply into his most fruitful tree, that it
may bear more fruit.

The words from the whirlwind invite Job to believe,
for the Lord discloses himself as he names the mysteries
in his world. Faith can't be commanded or coerced; it is
elicited by revelation. In seeing the Lord one sees oneself.

The way to feel small is to stand by someone who is tall. In the words of A. B. Davidson from *The Book of Job:*

> The object of the Lord's answer out of the whirlwind is twofold, to rebuke Job and to heal him—to bring home to his heart the blameworthiness of his words and demeanor toward God, and to lift him out of perplexity into peace. The two things hardly differ; at least both are affected by the same means, namely by God's causing all his glory to pass before Job.

What shall I answer?

Then Job answered the Lord: "Behold, I am
of small account; what shall I answer thee?"
(40:3-4a).

This is the moment Job has cried for, taunting the
Lord in an effort to hasten confrontation. This is the
audience Job has demanded, the stage he has longed for.
Now the floor is his.

Job has boasted that he will stand as a prince before
the Lord, for he has so much to say. He has vowed that
he will marshal irrefutable arguments, that he will march
against the unjust one with eloquent words. This is to be
his moment of self-vindication, when he claims the dignity
of the last word. He has composed his speech and re-
hearsed it well, but now he has lost his notes. The "greatest of all the people of the east" stands speechless and
confesses that he is of small account.

Job is stunned—stunned by the glory of God!

Ready for rescue

"I lay my hand on my mouth . . ." *(40:4b)*.

Laying one's hand upon one's mouth is to confess error. When Job lays his hand upon his mouth, letting himself be put in the wrong, he is finally profoundly right. His counselors have harangued him in an effort to increase his concern for his salvation. They have pressed him to raise the wrong question, What must I do to be saved? Now, in the face of God, he sees the question's irrelevance.

To encounter the God who offers his very self, and to receive him, is to move beyond concern to a trusting unconcern for one's salvation. By turning Job toward himself, his counselors urged him to stronger resolve, but his predicament calls not for resolve but for rescue.

Before God we are always in the wrong, but in our sin-blindedness we cannot see our guilt. Faith-inspired unconcern permits us to cast ourselves trustingly on the grace and mercy of the righteous one. This is love's break-in. It turns nobodies into somebodies, making us the people of God.

No further

"I lay my hand upon my mouth. I have spoken once, and I will not answer; twice, but I will proceed no further" (40:4b-5).

The Lord has attacked Job with throat-stuffing, tongue-tying questions, for Job has been a stubborn child. Now, to Job's everlasting credit, he lays his hand upon his mouth, responding with appropriate silence.

Some examinations are designed to give opportunity for a display of knowledge. This one calls for a blank paper. Its intention is to elicit wordless wonder. Yet its purpose isn't to humiliate but to heal.

Wonder is the first step toward health in the presence of the truly wonderful. Wonder can't be verbalized. The most beautiful music is silence, and our best liturgies leave all sound behind. For Job, this is an "O God!" moment. Before his friends he spoke eloquently; in the presence of the Lord he is dumb.

Perhaps prayer is at its best when it trails off into silence. May it not be that real prayer begins at the point where life is only an inarticulate cry? Certainly many of us have experienced, whether in anguish or in ecstasy, the "O, God" moment, too full of depth and pathos to be shared.

In *Man Is Not Alone*, A. J. Heschel speaks of wonder:

> Always we are chasing words and always words recede. But the greatest experiences are those

for which we have no expression. To live only on that which we can say is to wallow in the dust. . . . The most intimate is the most mysterious. Wonder alone is the compass that may direct us to the pole of meaning. To become aware of the ineffable is to part company with words. The essence, the tangent of the curve of human experience, lies beyond the limits of language. The world of things we perceive is but a veil. Its flutter is music, its ornament science, but what it conceals is inscrutable. Its silence remains unbroken; no words can carry it away. Sometimes we wish the world would cry and tell us about that which made it pregnant with fear-filling grandeur. Sometimes we wish our own heart would speak of that which made it heavy with wonder.

Questioned again

Then God answered Job out of the whirlwind:
"Gird up your loins like a man; I will question
you, and you declare to me" (40:6-7).

Now the poet seems to be passing a proper stopping place. It seems at first that the Book of Job should end here. God has asked for silence and Job has responded with his hand on his mouth. The Lord's purpose appears to be achieved. With his blank paper before him, Job is prepared to take his zero and say, "Can I go now?" But there is a goal yet to be reached.

Love isn't satisfied with silence. It wants to know and be known; it seeks to understand and be understood. The Lord's purpose with Job is to move beyond silence to a rebirth of fellowship and communion, a new level of living together and a new depth of oneness.

The Lord's display of knowledge and wisdom is a step, but not the final stage, in the healing of Job's fevered spirit. Not a hand upon the mouth, but a mouth re-opened for praise, a tongue freed for celebrative song— this is the goal of love in the lives of all who suffer.

An arm like God

"Will you even put me in the wrong? Will you
condemn me that you may be justified? Have
you an arm like God, and can you thunder with
a voice like his? Deck yourself with majesty and
dignity. Then will I also acknowledge to you,
that your own right hand can give you victory"
(from 40:8-14).

The Lord has centered Job's attention on the mysteries
in the natural order. Now there is a partial shift to the
moral order, with emphasis on God's omnipotence.

The power to think and the power to do—these human
endowments offer the greatest temptation to pride. They
invite the rebel to "go it alone." So now the God who
controls the course of history, who gives life and recalls
it, who proscribes boundaries beyond which the most
heavily armed wickedness cannot move, the God whose
eternal presence spans all generations and presides throughout the centuries, this God challenges the spindle-legged
pretenses of his servant Job. He asks him to show the
muscle which qualifies him to save himself.

Behold Behemoth!

"Behold, Behemoth, which I made as I made you; he eats grass like an ox. Behold, his strength in his loins, and his power in the muscles of his belly. He makes his tail stiff like a cedar; the sinews of his thighs are knit together. His bones are tubes of bronze, his limbs like bars of iron. Behold, if the river is turbulent he is not frightened; he is confident though Jordan rushes against his mouth. Can one take him with hooks, or pierce his nose with a snare?" (from 40:15-24).

Calling to mind the sheer bulk and brute strength of the hippopotamus, the Lord drives hard at Job's arrogance and lets him feel his puniness.

It is hard for one who has known command to relinquish authority. It is unpleasant to be forced to face one's helplessness and ultimate dependence. It takes spiritual surgery to face one's pride toward a fellow creature which is not frightened though the river is turbulent and is "confident though the Jordan rushes against his mouth."

But the Lord's purpose is always to turn his children toward himself, so now he points Job, for his comfort and strengthening, toward God's all-sufficient power and love.

Who can stand?

*"Can you draw out Leviathan with a fishhook,
or press down his tongue with a cord? Will he
make supplications to you? Will he speak to
you soft words? Will you play with him as
with a bird, or will you put him on leash for
your maidens? Lay hands on him, think of the
battle; you will not do it again! Upon earth
there is not his like, a creature without fear.
He beholds everything that is high; he is king
over all the sons of pride"* (from 41:1-34).

With irony and humor the Lord now turns Job's attention from the fearless hippopotamus to the equally fearless and more ferocious crocodile. Blending mythology with zoology, he describes an unconquerable creature—"king over all the sons of pride." But once again the spotlight turns on God: "Who then is he that can stand before me? Who has given to me, that I should repay him? Whatever is under the whole heaven is mine."

The Creator is beholden to none of his creatures. The breath of life is in his hand. By his bounty everything lives, be it hippopotamus, crocodile, or human being. For Job this becomes an irrefutable reminder that, just as he doesn't toy with the crocodile or put it on a leash, so he mustn't contemplate trying to contain the divine purpose and will. God is power and love—and truth. And truth is never a toy!

Throughout this questioning we are impressed with the severity of love. Love's eyes flash before any threat to the beloved. Love can't be mercy unless it has authority, and it is mercy that Job—ancient and contemporary—most needs.

Thou canst
do all things!

*Then Job answered the Lord: "I know that
thou canst do all things, and that no purpose of
thine can be thwarted. 'Who is this that hides
counsel without knowledge?' Therefore I have
uttered what I did not understand, things too
wonderful for me, which I did not know"
(42:1-3).*

"I know that thou canst do all things. . . ." Job has
been turned in upon himself, captive to his pain and
frustration. Now, like a weary traveler in a sturdy bed,
he comes to rest as frenzied inquiry gives way to confession and affirmation. His troubled heart has been drawn
to its home.

Freed from self-preoccupation, Job speaks a new language. The madness of self-justification gives way to free
and spontaneous praise of God. Job picks up the words
of the Lord, "Who is this that hides counsel without
knowledge?" He turns them against himself with an un-
equivocal plea of "guilty," acknowledging that his fevered
spirit has broken forth in pride and judgment.

Job has waited for an opportunity to press his integrity
and defend his righteousness. But now his words are few.
Like a small child, he has forgotten his piece. The majesty
of the moment has made him speechless. Before God's
righteousness there is no claim; before his love there is no
need to make one.

But now!

*"I had heard of thee by the hearing of the ear,
but now my eye sees thee"* (42:5).

This great moment in Job's encounter with the Lord strikes hard at the pragmatic theology of the winner, which tries to fit God into a uniform and draft him to give success to whatever one's latest idolatry demands.

Job doesn't pull God over to his side. He doesn't pray his way through to some self-chosen goal. He doesn't force God into his own pocket.

Only God can walk with us in the rubble and heal in the midst of loss. Only the cross can give hope, for without death there can be no rising. Dietrich Bonhoeffer said that the call to discipleship is a call to come and die. Job has throughout the book been called to such discipleship. Having witnessed the collapse of all that has visibly supported him, he can say, "But now my eye sees thee." This is Job's *Yes*—the ultimate turnabout that brings peace.

Now I see!

*"I had heard of thee by the hearing of the ear,
but now my eye sees thee" (42:5)*

For the first time, Job sees all things "new," including himself. In the face of God, Job sees his own face. God-knowledge yields authentic self-knowledge.

Because Job hasn't known the Lord or himself fully, in his suffering, he has felt like nothing more than a driven leaf or a bit of stubble. He has felt forsaken. But when God's majesty "stops to talk" and God's loving power bends low to touch him, he sees himself as the cherished person he is. He becomes reacquainted with himself as he looks into the heart of his Creator. His equilibrium is restored and his craving to understand is swallowed up in the joy of belonging. God's presence is his peace.

This moment of revelation is the Thomas moment. The cry of recognition isn't just "O Lord," but "My Lord and my God!" Questions are swallowed up in counter-questions—or the touch of a hand.

In the Cambridge Bible, A. B. Davidson says:

> The solution to Job's problem given in God's answer from the storm is a religious solution, not a speculative one. It is a solution to the heart, not to the intellect. It is such a solution as only God can give, a solution which does not solve the perplexity but buries it under the tide of a fuller life and joy in God. It is a solution as broad as Job's life and not merely the mea-

> sure of his understanding, the same solution as
> was given to the doubting apostle, making him
> to exclaim, "My Lord and My God!" and
> teaching him that not through his sense or his
> eyesight, but through a broader sense, God
> makes himself felt by man (pp. 298-299).

Just as the Lord's address from the whirlwind reshapes Job's concerns and attitudes, so suffering sometimes spurs us to reassess our values and make painful reappraisals. All the answers Job has clamored for don't blow in with the storm, but some of his questions blow out. Job's perspective shifts with divine encounter. His questions no longer claim primary urgency. When he finally opens his mouth, it isn't to question but to confess and affirm.

When one comes with prefabricated questions into the presence of a great master of any art, the best that can be hoped for is to so encounter that person that one must later say of all the questions, "I forgot to ask!"

In dust and ashes

*"Therefore I despise myself, and repent
in dust and ashes" (42:6).*

We have arrived at the spiritual summit of the book,
the joy-in-heaven moment. The prince becomes captive to
forgiving love. This is the ultimate test of Job's integrity,
his response to the presence and person of God. It is the
universal test in which the brittle break and the humble
bend.

Humility is basically honesty. And Job is honest. He
"comes forth as gold"; the caldron hasn't destroyed him.
Contrary to Satan's slander, Job "holds fast his integrity."

Job is satisfied, not because of possessions or position
or anything outside himself. His purse is flat but his
person is full. He is restored at the depth of his being,
beyond the reach of any human hand. It is enough. The
bridge from abandonment to vindication of hope is complete. "Blessed are the poor in spirit." The King has
opened the kingdom.

"Therefore I despise myself, and repent." Job is expe-
riencing wonder, the wonder of an Isaiah crying, "Woe
is me"; the wonder of a Peter pleading, "Depart from me,
for I am a sinful man"; the wonder of proud Saul becoming the "little one." Job has asked the answer to a
riddle; God gives him victory in a battle. The highest that
Job can think or ask can't satisfy him. The solution and

131

the question have to come from outside and beyond him. Grace is his need, grace in the form of God.

Job repents. This is his response to the sense of being asked, and this is the heart of his experience of wonder. In the words of A. J. Heschel:

> Wonder is not a state of esthetic enjoyment. Endless wonder is endless tension, a situation in which we are shocked at the inadequacy of our awe, at the weakness of our shock, as well as the state of being asked the ultimate question. Endless wonder unlocks the innate sense of indebtedness. Within our awe there is no place for self-assertion. Within our awe we only know that all we own we owe. The world consists not of things, but of tasks. Wonder is the state of being asked *(Man Is Not Alone)*.

Therefore I repent

"Therefore I despise myself,
and repent in dust and ashes" (42:6).

"The action of Job abhoring himself and repenting is significant not for any motives in Job, but for its movement toward Someone beyond Job. The mere presence of God is sufficient to command or explain God's action" (Eugene Goodheart, from *Twentieth Century Interpretations of the Book of Job,* Paul S. Sanders, ed.).

Job is satisfied, not in fresh conquest, but in renewed surrender; not in stronger pursuit, but in more complete capture. He gives himself up to the grace and wisdom of God. We walk with Job, not into more complete explanations, but into larger appropriations of grace.

God overcomes Job's anguish and fear of living, not by settling him down, but by rousing him and drawing him further into the risks of faith. The mystery of the good sun-blinded Job. Caught up and captured even a little by this mystery, we enlarge our understanding of the place of wonder in the life of trust.

Wonder isn't an esthetic treat or spiritual sweet, peripheral to faith. Wonder is central to faith's venture. It is the rapture of the trusting spirit, ready for the disciple's errand. It breaks one open to new commissioning. It increases the range of readiness. It never leaves one the same but lifts all things to a higher level of regard. Wonder suggests newness; it ushers in the morning mood.

Wonder involves arrest, apprehension, and complete capture, leading to recognition and then to capitulation. It suggests that we can be held accountable, for we are responsible. We can't beg to be excused.

Wonder is an emotional and volitional frontier. It leads to broader and deeper levels of commitment and life-participation. It invites those who trust to increased creativity and exploration into God's glory and grace.

Mission accomplished

"I had heard of thee by the hearing of the ear,
but now my eye sees thee; therefore I despise
myself, and repent in dust and ashes" (42:5-6)

The Lord has spoken. He has lifted back the veil and Job has seen. He is no longer the prince. He is the child, wide-eyed and open-mouthed, conditioned not for investigation but for celebration. Job worships. The Lord's mission is accomplished and Job is satisfied. His spirit is at home—home at last!

Such an outcome torpedoes bland and easy thoughts on prayer. At this point, Job's story hasn't come out right. He is still stripped of possessions, power, and loved ones. How can he be at peace with the Lord and himself when he hasn't "gotten what he came for."

But he has been given something better. What he heard "by the hearing of the ear" can't compare with what he now sees and "understands." He is still far from understanding God's justice, but his priorities have been rearranged. He is no longer interested in playing God. His urgencies have shifted.

The question Why do I suffer? is not asked again. Like a pebble dropped into a canyon, his big questions, in the words of R. B. Sewall, "echo into nothingness in the infinite mystery and the glory." There are no easy answers on the subject of God's government of his world. When we feel completely at ease about our attitudes toward prayer, they usually need rethinking and reassessment.

I once encouraged mistaken ideas about prayer. I said that decisions prayed over would be right decisions; that children loved, prayed over, and instructed with wisdom and care would surely be spared catastrophic losses and injuries. I no longer believe this. I do fervently believe in prayer, but I don't assess its efficacy by how God's answers correspond to my individual petitions. I believe that God is lovingly adequate and all-sufficient, and that "he's got the whole world in his hands."

In a recent discussion of this matter with a friend, I was led to say: "Do you know that if I should have tried to tie God to discernable answers to my little prayers—'please let this happen; please don't let that happen!'—in recent months I would most probably have stopped praying?" He replied, "What do you pray for then?"

I told him of a friend of many years ago. This friend gave me many good gifts, and one great one. The great one was a thought on the subject of prayer which I have cherished ever since. He had gone through a period of "Job's losses," including the loss of health. We sat together, neither saying much, for we were looking into the face of mystery. I remember that silence. It was he who broke it when he said, "My prayer is that nothing of this may be lost upon us."

136

I have borrowed this prayer, "that nothing of this may be lost upon us," scores of times in the intervening years. This wonderfully durable thought is a summary of the fittest response to Job's encounter with the Lord of the whirlwind.

There is an ecology of grace, a store of "God-born energy" that mustn't be lost upon us. Surely no pollution is so ominous as pollution of the good news by legalistic and moralistic interpretations, no waste so threatening as the waste of God's overtures to callous and unbelieving people. Job sees and repents, a witness to faith, a model of the trusting spirit.

The final impact of the whirlwind experience upon Job is: "Immanuel, God with us." Immanuel is the God of Job. The night is not strange to Immanuel; he knows every lone traveler in it. Therefore, faith's report from every lonely outpost is still this, "The Star, the Star! I still see the Star, the Star to guide me and the Star to share!"

My wrath is kindled

"After the Lord has spoken
these words to Job . . ." (42:7).

The Lord has drawn Job to himself by a revelation of
his glory and majesty, offering Job's driven spirit the
haven his heart craved. Now God deals with his defenders,
Eliphaz, Bildad, and Zophar. These three haven't been
open to surprise as Job has. They haven't trusted the
Lord enough to dare sharing Job's frightening inquiry. In
championing their interpretations of God's ways, they
have been hostile toward their lonely, tormented brother.

Perhaps the Lord's wrath says that he wants, not defense, but loving and courageous witness, proclamation of
his sometimes-hidden grace. He asks for staunch heralds
of his goodness, of his loving concern for the sufferer. The
Lord isn't served in the hurting ways these three have dealt
with Job, no matter how zealously righteous their in-
tentions.

The Lord has offered these men opportunity to change
with Job, to enlarge their perspective. He has invited them,
through Job, to larger risks of faith, but they have drawn
back. In drawing back, they not only reject Job, but also
harass and attack him.

Go to my servant

*"Now therefore take seven bulls and seven rams,
and go to my servant Job, and offer up for
yourselves a burnt offering; and my servant Job
shall pray for you, for I will accept his prayer
not to deal with you according to your folly;
for you have not spoken of me what is right,
as my servant Job has"* (42:8).

Three times the Lord hangs the garland of honor upon
Job with the repetition of the title "my servant."

Eliphaz, Bildad, and Zophar have put Job down. They
have towered over him in lordly superiority, combining
their weight against him.

Now the Sovereign One turns the tables granting to
Job in their very presence a decisive reinstatement.

The Lord places the errant friends in the position of
need, appointing Job their mediator and priest. Job stands
as high priest, the suffering one who intercedes for those
who torment him.

More than
his beginning

And the Lord restored the fortunes of Job,
when he had prayed for his friends; and the
Lord gave Job twice as much as he had before.
And the Lord blessed the latter days of Job
more than his beginning (42:10, 12).

The prose prolog and epilog form the classic framework of the Book of Job. The prolog presents a lofty model, distant and untouchable. The poem brings us a warm, real-life brother who speaks to all people. The quality of despair we encounter in the person of Job makes the book international and universal. The book is not for heroes but for saints, as it moves more and more in the direction of proving God's right to be God.

The prose epilog is hardly needed by us who read the book on this side of Easter. There are those who say that it spoils the book, taking the edge off it and vitiating its impact by being untrue to life. It is untrue to life if we force it to speak only in material, literal terms.

But we must let the book speak its truth in its own way. In symbolic language the epilog says that God is in command even while outward circumstances seem out of hand, and that God never permits loss except to make room for greater gain. This doesn't mean that he settles accounts on the twentieth of each month, or that losses and gains are "in kind." It means that he is the God who recreates and restores, and that his design is patterned in love.

Reading from the Christian perspective, the eschatological, we affirm that every temporal loss must be assessed against a heavenly gain. However, if the book was to address its day with its limited view of life beyond the grave, the epilog served to complete the message of the book, "that sufferings are for the righteous man the way to glory, and that his faith is the way to sight."

Full of days

And the Lord restored the fortunes of Job,
when he prayed for his friends; and the Lord
gave Job twice as much as he had before. And
Job died, an old man, and full of days
(42:10, 17).

Job's prayer for those who have "despitefully used him" is his eloquent act of acceptance and forgiveness. Now Job is sent to others. The servant is asked to serve, and he doesn't hold back. The loud protestations and hungry questions from the ash heap now become a prayer for his friends. Job's readiness to forgive overflows from his own forgiveness.

The grace of God will not be kept. It is personal but not private. Forgiveness, like water, seeks its own level. It reaches out to the unforgiven, for love is never static. Its benedictions won't be contained; its riches can't be hoarded.

"Then came to him all his brothers and sisters, and all who had known him before." Their "piece of money and ring of gold" is a safe gift, the ludicrous "too little and too late" of the guilty conscience. Job's pockets are suddenly full of hush money, paid by those who did not heed Job's call in his time of need.

The ill-timed and shabby collections which we, too, persist in, are an insult to those who need us. Late gifts—self-serving and ego-aggrandizing—are a gross form of

142

selfishness. The Book of Job doesn't buttress faith in human beings. It shows them as the fickle lovers they are. Job must have inwardly both wept and smiled as he indulged this self-display of family and friends.

"Prosperity now brought those together again whom calamity had frightened away; for the love of men is scarcely anything but a number of coarse and delicate shades of selfishness" (Delitsch, p. 389).

"And the Lord blessed the latter days of Job more than his beginning. . . . He had also seven sons and three daughters." Perhaps this is resurrection language—twice as much property as before, but still only seven sons and three daughters. Is the sacred writer reminding us that faith never loses a loved one, and that nothing can separate from the love and care of the God who has authority to say "my servant"?

From the prose prolog to the epilog there is a full circle from "my servant Job" and back to "my servant." God says "mine." This is the heart of the Book of Job. Here the battle between the adversary and God is permanently pitched.

And so it is in my life. There is a "cosmic event" in my history, my Baptism. God has said, "mine," and now he invites me to trust him. This is the point of greatest temptation, that of letting the devil destroy my sense of belonging and permitting him to rob me of my name.

The shape of the question is always, Whose am I? Who

am I? All issues hang on this. The ethical crisis is really a crisis of belonging, a crisis in identity. One thing is hung so high that it is out of reach of the long finger of changing circumstance, and that is the fact that God says "mine." He holds me. He possesses me. This is my mighty fortress.

It is apparent after even so brief a study of this book that it is no one's ready handbook. It isn't instant wisdom, instant comfort, or instant insight for troubled times. It isn't a floodlight overhead, or even a flashlight in the hand. Rather, it suggests starlight.

The story is not mainly about people dealing with people, and the book isn't a "what-to-do" book for those who want to help. It is rather a "who-to-be" book for persons who want to live authentically with themselves and others. The central theme is more than that of people dealing with troubled peers. It is God offering his very self to the undeserving.

"After this Job lived a hundred and forty years, and saw his sons, and his sons' sons, four generations. And Job died, an old man, and full of days." Richer through loss, stronger through test, truly "there was a man," a man whose home was in the light, but who came to know full well the color of the night. His name was Job.